Encouragement in the Trenches of Motherhood

60 Daily Devotions to

Inspire Moms to Live Intentionally

Dedicated to my Savior,

Jesus Christ, who has made this possible. All glory goes to Him. Also, to my wonderful husband and children.

ISBN: 979-8-218-55029-5

Table of Contents

From My Heart to Yours

The kids were finally in bed, so I flopped onto the sofa with my book. As usual, I'd been busy all day with my four young children, but I felt like I hadn't really accomplished anything. I had yelled at my children way more than I cared to admit. My bathroom probably hadn't been cleaned in a month, and when I paused, I noticed piles stacked everywhere. I certainly didn't feel up to tackling them at this point in the day. I knew things had to change.

This was not the life I had imagined. Once upon a time, I was a young girl dreaming of becoming a farmer's wife! Sometimes I dreamed of training horses. But taking a moment to reflect on these dreams, I suppose it may be true that seldom does life go exactly the way a girl imagines.

I married later than I had expected . . . a handsome military man, not a farmer. We moved eight times over twenty years as we raised our six beautiful children. We mourned twin girls, lost shortly after their birth, along with at least six miscarried babies. We gathered countless wonderful friendships as we trekked across the country. Along with braving seven deployments, we proudly celebrated twenty years of marriage.

In the midst of those big milestones, during a rare moment of clarity, I realized I wasn't designed to drown in chaos and grief. I knew in my heart that God had a bigger purpose for motherhood than only changing diapers, cooking food, and cleaning my home. I tried on the idea of a new direction. What would it be like to be a mom with purpose? This warmed my heart and gave me a feeling of direction.

I knew I couldn't possibly be alone in my thinking, so I began to search blogs, read books, ask organized mom friends for help, and slowly tried out a few of their suggestions. I started to find my own way. Over time, small changes turned into more small changes, which resulted in big changes. It took time, but eventually I was no longer drowning.

I haven't always dreamed of writing a devotional. Actually, I haven't always dreamed of many of the things I'm currently doing! But God. God had other plans.

Several years ago, I started to feel that God was telling me it was time to step up. I was no longer a young mom, and I should be helping and encouraging other moms. Around that same time, for some reason (God), I listened to a webinar on starting a blog. The lady said, "The thing holding people back is starting, so just start!"

Well, since I had thought for a while that a blog might be cool, I started my blog, Mama Reflections, a day or two later. It took me a while to get going, since I was way over my head on the technical side. I wanted to encourage moms on the motherhood journey, so I kept pressing forward. My heart was led to teach them the things that have made the biggest difference during my journey from overwhelm and burnout to peace and purpose as a mom.

After I got the blog going, I began to have the thought of writing a mom's devotional. While I did create a Bible reading plan for moms, I knew a devotional would be a much bigger project.

In the meantime, I grew my blog by writing new posts, which ended up reaching thousands of women who wanted to hear more about being a mom with purpose. After getting more skilled with blogging, I decided to begin coaching Christian moms through a "signature program" I was able to develop: From Chaos to Peace. I was starting to be able to help overwhelmed Christian moms in tangible ways. To keep up with what I'm currently doing, be sure to join my email list at Mama Reflections.

Finally, after several years, this mom devotional has come to fruition! I've been able to use what I've gleaned from my own nineteen years of experience being a mom, coaching other moms, and what I've learned from moms who have joined my Facebook group, Christian Moms Living On Purpose, to make sure I'm covering the topics, challenges, and questions moms just like you are struggling with. In this devotional, my heart is to encourage you to embrace the motherhood journey with intentionality and purpose. Ultimately, I'm praying that you will grow your relationship with Jesus through this tool.

With lots of Love,
Aimee Niblack
Mom | Coach | Mentor | Blogger

How to Use This Devotional

I'm so excited that you have chosen to embark on this journey with me! Whether you are a new Christian or have been following Jesus for a long time, this devotional is designed to encourage and inspire you to live more fully in the motherhood calling God has given you.

I've been a follower of Jesus for forty years and a Christian mom for nearly nineteen years. With six children, I know how difficult it can be to take time to spend with God. You try to get up early for some quiet time with God, but your preschooler and toddler wake up and need your attention. Here are some tips I've learned over the years:

- Grab a friend for accountability to keep you motivated.
- Choose the time of day that will work best.
- Set aside at least 10-20 minutes of time. (With children, it will not always be uninterrupted, but it's good for them to see you carve out time for God.)
- Pray and ask God to learn what He would have you learn.
- Have a pen and notebook (if you don't want to write in this devotional book).

How it works

This devotional has three main sections with subtopics under each. Each subtopic is broken up into five days with a bonus coloring page for each section! The daily sections contain a Bible passage or two along with a key verse. Reading the whole passage is highly encouraged so you can get the most out of it. This will also help you see the context of the passage.

After each daily section, you will find reflection questions with space included to write your answers, followed by a short prayer. Designed with the busy mom in mind, each daily devotional will take approximately ten to fifteen minutes to study and complete. You can take longer if you would like to take more time journaling and praying through that day's Scripture and questions.

While I encourage you to go through the devotional in order, you may also choose to jump to a particular topic of struggle. If you do this, please try to read through that topic section in order. Once you've finished that topic section, go back to the beginning and use the devotional straight through to fully benefit from the flow of topics in this devotional.

The coloring page for each section is designed to give you time to reflect on what God has taught you in that section. It's most effective if you color the reflection page *after* you finish all the daily sections related to the topic. Take the time as you color to pray and reflect on what you've learned. I'd love for this to be a meaningful part of your experience as you grow in each area.

Starting a devotional is easy, but finishing one can be challenging. That's why I started a community of Christian moms to encourage one another in our faith journey. I invite you to join my Christian Moms Living on Purpose Facebook group to share your devotional journey with me and other Christian moms.

What's included?

This devotional contains sixty days of daily devotions written specifically for moms in the midst of raising their children. There is space inside the devotional to journal your thoughts to the reflection questions. Each topic section includes a bonus coloring page as a reflection and prayer tool, and I've even included some small group discussion questions in the back of the book.

Use for a small group

This devotional can be used for a small mom's group. Simply gather a few friends to join in. Each week, read one section on your own, before getting together to talk through the reflection questions. You can also add some of the small group questions included at the back. This can be a perfect way to build a community of Christian women to encourage you in the journey as you talk through these topics! For more resources on how to run your small group for moms, visit my website at https://mamareflections.com/encouragement-in-the-trenches-of-motherhood-small-groups

Godly Motherhood

As followers of Christ, we need to be the kind of moms God has called us to be. In this section, I want to cover some topics that are important to address in order to grow as a godly mom. These are areas that many moms struggle with, including me, so know that you are not alone. That said, God wants to grow you in each area. Will you let Him? Are you ready?

Identity in Christ

- *Day 1: I am Loved*

- *Day 2: I am a Child of God*

- *Day 3: I am Not Condemned*

- *Day 4: I am Wonderfully Made*

- *Day 5: I am Cared For*

I **Am** who **God** says that I **Am**

Day 1: I am Loved

~ Read: Romans 5:1-11: John 3:16 ~

"but God shows his love for us in that while we were still sinners, Christ died for us."
Romans 5:8

I am loved. Let that sink in. These words are the heart of the gospel.

I recently asked my small women's Bible study to explain the gospel. A majority of them couldn't (or wouldn't in case they got it wrong) do it. As Christian moms, we need to know, believe, and be able to communicate the gospel of Jesus, especially to our children. Sometimes, we make it more complicated than it needs to be.

Our Scripture verses today remind us of the truth of the gospel. We are reminded that God loved us so much that He sent His Son to die in our place, and that whoever believes in Him will have eternal life. They remind us not only that Christ died, but that He died for us while we were still sinners. You don't have to improve or change before trusting in Jesus as your Savior. He is the One who does the changing in your life.

Because of Jesus and Jesus alone, you are justified and released from your sin and freed from the wrath of God. Only because of Jesus are you reconciled to God. Only because of Jesus has your debt been paid. Only because of Jesus are you made righteous.

Remember, the gospel message is not a one-and-done thing. The gospel is what continues to change us every day. It is a living gift that changes how we interact with our families and the world around us. As you embrace what Jesus did for you, you can share this Good News with others, especially your family.

If you have not yet placed your faith and trust in Jesus for salvation, come to Him. Simply talk to Him, confessing that you believe He died in your place, that He conquered death by rising again, and that you want to make Him Lord of your life. He loves you more than you can imagine. Mama, you are loved!

Reflection Questions:

How is love the heart of the gospel?

_____

_____

_____

Summarize the gospel in your own words.

_____

_____

_____

Have you placed your faith in Jesus for salvation? Share your testimony. If you haven't, what is holding you back?

_____

_____

_____

Prayer:

"Heavenly Father, thank you for providing the way of salvation through Jesus. Thank you, Jesus, for the love You have shown by taking on God's wrath for my sin. Help me to embrace the gospel message each and every day. Help me to be able to share it with my children and those around me. In Jesus's name I pray, Amen."

Day 2: I am a Child of God

~ Read: John 1:11-13; 1 John 3:1-2 ~

"But to all who did receive him, who believed in his name, he gave the right to become children of God."

John 1:12

We all have our favorite possessions. It may be a favorite sweater or a pair of comfy shoes. Perhaps yours is something more sentimental. Like mine is a blueberry mug that was my favorite grandma's.

However, as a mom, you know these favorite possessions are nothing quite like the moment you first held your baby in your arms. I remember the awe at how fragile this little human was, but also the reality that this little one is so dependent upon me. I never realized how in love I could be. True for you, too?

When you think back over those favorite possessions, your child comes out ahead by far! As much as you love your child, do you realize that you are God's child, and He loves you even more? He is perfect and so His love is perfect.

You aren't His child because of how good you are, how pretty you are, how organized you are, or how much you have it together. It's a good thing, right? We are all a mess in certain areas of our lives! You are God's child simply because you believe in His name and trust in Him for your salvation. You believe He did what He said. You know He is God; the only One who could save us. You know that His sacrifice on the cross was enough.

Since you are a child of God, you also have the benefits of being His child. You have His love and forgiveness, His mercy and grace. You know that He is listening to your prayers. You know that your home is secured in heaven.

As God's child, you also have the Holy Spirit residing in you. He helps you understand the Bible, convicts you of sin, to lovingly guide you and help you know how to live. He gives you the strength for each day. You are a child of God, and that's amazing!

Reflection questions:

When you think of how you love your child/children, what words come to mind?

_____

_____

_____

What does it mean to you that you are a child of God?

_____

_____

_____

What does it mean to you that you don't have to earn God's favor to be His child? (See Ephesians 2:8; Romans 5:8)

_____

_____

_____

_____

Prayer:

"Dear Lord, I am so thankful to be called Your child. I realize that I did nothing to deserve it, but You love me anyway. Nothing can separate me from Your love. Amen."

Day 3: I am Not Condemned

~ Read: Romans 8:1-11 ~

"There is therefore now no condemnation for those who are in Christ Jesus."
Romans 8:1

Lisa screamed at her girls to stop fighting, yet again. They didn't listen. In a huff, she picked up each one and plopped them in their beds. "Stay there until I say you can get out!"

As she went back to the kitchen, her mind spiraled as it often did after she lost her temper. Why do I keep losing my temper? I told myself I would never be angry like my mom was, but here I am doing the same thing. I'm such a failure! How can I ever get this right?

Do you know what? Lisa is living in condemnation. She feels that since she keeps messing up, God can't or won't forgive her. Go back and read the key verse again. If you are in Christ, there is NO condemnation.

You are no longer in the flesh but are in the Spirit. Do you know what that means? God can change you, even when you can't change yourself. He lives in you and is working in you. I know that sometimes the growth process seems way too slow for our liking, but growth is happening. The truth is, when God looks at you, He sees the righteousness of Jesus! You are as pure as snow.

If you are continuing to feel guilty for your sin, know that there is no condemnation in Christ. Ask Him for forgiveness and know that He will no longer remember it! Live in that truth. You are NOT condemned, and that is such great news!

Reflection Questions:

In what areas do you find yourself living under condemnation?

_____

_____

_____

How does this passage remind you of what is true instead?

_____

_____

_____

What practical step can you take to remind yourself that there is no condemnation in Christ?

_____

_____

_____

Prayer:

"Father God, You have said that there is no condemnation for those who are in Christ. I see that I have been believing the lie that I am still condemned because I continue to fail. Thank You for your forgiveness. Thank You that You are growing me into who You want me to be. Amen."

Day 4: I am Wonderfully Made

~ Read: Psalm 139 ~

"For you formed my inward parts; you knitted me together in my mother's womb. I praise you, for I am fearfully and wonderfully made. Wonderful are your works; my soul knows it very well."
Psalm 139:13-14

Comparison is everywhere. You scroll on social media and wonder why your home doesn't look like that. You see the fitness moms with their seemingly perfect bodies and wish you could find time and energy to work out. Then you show up at your local mom's group and compare your messy bun and leggings to the mom at your table wearing a cute top, makeup, and perfect hair. You've been struggling with imperfection, but now you feel like a failure.

Can I let you in on a secret? None of those moms have it all together. They are sure to be struggling in some less visible area. I know that feeling: that was me. On the outside, I had it together. I never left the house without cute clothes, makeup, and hair. But do you know what? My house was a disaster and I was constantly running late. Also, I was yelling at my kids more than I would ever admit.

When you are struggling with comparison, you need this reminder. You are fearfully and wonderfully made. YOU are fearfully and wonderfully made. You ARE fearfully and wonderfully made. You are FEARFULLY and WONDERFULLY made.

God didn't make a mistake when He made you. He knew you would be the perfect mother for your children. He knew what you would be great at and what you would need to depend on Him for. God made you beautifully unique!

Reflection Questions:

Recall a time when you have struggled with comparison. What would God say to you about it?

_____

_____

_____

How does it help to know that you are fearfully and wonderfully made?

_____

_____

_____

How does knowing that God cares about the details of your life make a difference?

_____

_____

_____

Prayer:

"Heavenly Father, I get it now. I'm not like anyone else. You made me unique and special. I am fearfully and wonderfully made, and I praise You for that. Help me to embrace my strengths and lean on You in my weaknesses. Help me to stop comparing myself to others. Thank you for how You made me. Amen."

Day 5: I am Cared For

~ Read: 1 Peter 5:6-11; Matthew 6:25-34 ~

"Casting all your anxieties on him, because he cares for you."
1 Peter 5:7

With tears streaming down my cheeks, I placed the letter on the altar. It was what I had to give to Jesus that Christmas.

Our church had been encouraged to figure out a special gift for Jesus. After some thought and prayer, I knew this would be mine. The letter thanked Jesus for all the ways He was there for me during the premature rupture of membranes, ten weeks of bedrest, and subsequent loss of my twin girls, Gabrielle and Michelle.

I thanked Him for providing comfort and help from strangers and family alike. There were friends to pack our house and move us to our next location, a new friend to let me spend the night before a medical transport, and support from the military commanders. I had wonderful Christian nurses, church members in the new location to visit me in the hospital (they didn't even know me), family to care for our one-year-old daughter, and more!

If I ever doubt that God cares for me, I only have to remember this season. I remember how the body of Christ surrounded us before and after our losses. God was in the details and He worked in a personal way.

Satan would like nothing more than to lead you to believe otherwise, but God isn't just off in the distance, no longer caring for His creation. He continues to be involved in a personal way. He cares for even the birds and the lilies, and He sees and cares for YOU. Let Him know your worries and fears. He cares for every single one.

Reflection Questions:

What thoughts come to mind when someone says that God cares personally for YOU?

_____

_____

_____

_____

How does this passage give you comfort?

_____

_____

_____

_____

What truth from God's Word will you use to combat the lie that God doesn't care?

_____

_____

_____

_____

Prayer:

"Heavenly Father, I know that You care for the birds of the air and the lilies of the field, and You care even more for me. You will give me everything I need, so I cast all my worries and fears on You. Thank You that You care for ME. In Jesus's name I pray, Amen."

Increasing in Patience

- *Day 6: Why am I Impatient?*

- *Day 7: Stress and Lack of Patience*

- *Day 8: The Fruit of Patience*

- *Day 9: Growing in Patience*

- *Day 10: The Patient Mom*

Lord, teach me Patience

Day 6: Why Am I Impatient?

~ Read: Isaiah 26:1-12 ~

"You keep him in perfect peace whose mind is stayed on you, because he trusts in you."
Isaiah 26:3

Did you know that patience is one of the top struggles Christian moms deal with? I mean, have you ever lost your patience and yelled at your child? Yeah, me too! A lot!

While there are many reasons you could be feeling impatient, it seems to boil down to mainly a few. Can you guess what they are? The top few I see are stress or busyness, unmet behavior expectations, and pride. I have dealt with all three of these for sure!

Often we are way too busy, leading to way too much stress. Yes, raising children is a busy season of life, but we often make it worse by committing to extra things.

Lack of patience due to unmet behavior expectations happens when our children are not behaving in the way *we* think they should. Perhaps they are taking too long to get ready to leave the house, running around yelling in a store, or refusing to obey something you've just told them to do. You find yourself getting upset because they aren't meeting your expectations.

Pride is another common reason you may lose your patience. For example, you just settled your children in bed and settled down with your favorite tea with a new book. You hear talking and squealing coming from down the hallway. You may tell them kindly a few times to quiet down and go to sleep. But, by the 4th time you lose it! How dare they inconvenience you! Yup, been there.

Isaiah 26 is a great reminder of how we can be at peace when our mind is fixed on God. We can put our trust in Him and yearn for Him and His ways. When we are at peace with our minds fixed on God, we won't be impatient. We are more likely to be calm and careful with our words. Keep reading as we delve more into the topic of patience tomorrow.

Reflection Questions:

What struggles with patience do you have?

_____

_____

_____

Which of these three reasons for impatience seem to be most common for you?

_____

_____

_____

_____

How can you put Isaiah 26:3 into practice this week?

_____

_____

_____

_____

Prayer:
"Father God, I know I need to be more patient with my children. I can see why I'm often the opposite of that. Please help me to stay in perfect peace by fixing my mind on You. Help me to focus on You and what You have called me to do instead of on myself. Amen."

Day 7: Stress and Lack of Patience

~ Read: Matthew 11:28-30 ~

"Come to me, all who labor and are heavy laden, and I will give you rest."
Matthew 11:28

I walked into our playroom, tripping over toys as I went. I yelled at my kids for probably the fifth time to clean it up, but it was still a disaster! In fact, much of my home was the same way. My four kids were seven and under, and I just couldn't seem to keep up. I was constantly over-whelmed and stressed. I was losing patience and feeling like I was failing. Maybe you are feeling like this now.

Stress is a huge reason many of us moms (yes, this is a big one for me), lose our patience. You have way too much on your plate - children who need you, a home that you just can't seem to keep up with, and too many commitments and obligations. You are way too burned out. . . so you yell at your kids . . . over every. little. thing.

Can you relate?

Mama, Jesus is calling to you, "Come to Me." Will you listen? He will give you rest. Rest sounds much better than stress, doesn't it?

My pastor says that if you are too busy, overwhelmed, and stressed, then you must be doing something that God hasn't called you to do. Go ahead and read that again. What extra things are you doing or holding onto? Let go and gain your strength from the One who will give it to you.

As you let go of the extra burdens and lean on Jesus, you will find rest for your soul. As you find rest, you will have more patience for your husband and children.

Reflection Questions:

What is your relationship between stress and lack of patience?

_____

_____

_____

What is on your plate that doesn't need to be there?

_____

_____

_____

How will you find your rest in Christ?

_____

_____

_____

Prayer:

"Dear Lord, I am so tired. Tired of being stressed. Tired of losing my patience. Tired of being busy. Help me to find Your priorities for my life and only focus on them. Help me to let go of the things that don't matter. Give me the strength to do what You have called me to do in this season. Thank You! Amen."

Day 8: The Fruit of Patience

~ Read: Galatians 5:16-25 ~

"But the fruit of the Spirit is love, joy, peace, patience, kindness, goodness, faithfulness, gentleness, self-control; against such things there is no law."
Galatians 5:22-23

Before I was a mom, I would be critical of moms who had a screaming child. *I would never let my child do that. He needs a good spanking!* I would think. Then, I had THAT child! Nothing seemed to work with the tantrums! Nothing.

You go to great lengths to teach your children to be patient and not throw fits about everything that doesn't go their way. But, how often do *you* throw a fit when things don't go your way? How often do you lose your cool when they don't cooperate? As adults, our patience and self-control often isn't much better than our children's.

In the first part of our passage for today, we're reminded that if we walk according to the Spirit, we won't gratify those fleshly desires. Lack of patience and self-control are most certainly examples of fleshly desires.

As we live by the Spirit, we will keep in step with Him. As we live by the Spirit, the fruits of the Spirit will grow in our lives. We can't force the fruit to grow by our own strength. Fruit is a by-product of abiding in Christ, spending time in relationship with Him, and keeping in step with Him. As we tend the roots of our lives by abiding in Christ, the fruits will take care of themselves.

Remember, growing fruit isn't an overnight process. I know I often wish I'd grow in certain areas faster than I actually do. I have to remind myself that my job is to be faithful in my relationship with God. I encourage you to do the same, and change will come!

Reflection Questions:

Do you struggle with the fruit of patience in your life? What does that look like?

_____

_____

_____

How are you currently living by the Spirit versus the flesh?

_____

_____

_____

What is one way you can be faithful in growing in your relationship with Christ?

_____

_____

_____

_____

Prayer:

"Dear Lord, I get so upset when my children don't cooperate. I realize that I can't grow the fruit of patience and self-control by my own strength. Help me to live by the Spirit instead of the flesh. Help me to be faithful in my relationship with You. In Jesus's Name, Amen."

Day 9: Put on Patience

~ Read: Colossians 3 ~

"Put on then, as God's chosen ones, holy and beloved, compassionate hearts, kindness, humility, meekness, and patience,"
Colossians 3:12

A God coincidence, but my local Bible study covered Colossians 3:1-17 just this morning! We were reminded of what we were to put off and what to put on instead. In Christ, what we put on is our new identity.

A couple of weeks ago, we were talking about anger in my biblical counseling class. I realized that loss of patience is actually anger, which is one of the things Paul tells us to put off in our passage today. These earthly passions are to be put to death.

Death is very final. It doesn't say to minimize these sins or cut back on these sins. Instead, it says to put them to death. Put them away from you.

Does this mean we will never fail? No, but it does mean we need to be serious about wearing the attributes befitting you as God's chosen ones. You are now holy (set apart). You are now patient by the grace of God.

The passage goes on to tell us to put on love above all because love binds the rest together. When we are loving, we are not only patient, but kind, thankful, humble, and compassionate. When we are loving, we care more about the well-being of others than having our own way. That love will help us put on patience.

Reflection Questions:

What are your thoughts on lack of patience really being anger?

_____

_____

_____

How can you put off anger in your life?

_____

_____

_____

How can you instead put on love and patience this week?

_____

_____

_____

Prayer:

"Dear Lord, I confess that I have been only trying to minimize lack of patience in my life, but I realize I need to actually put anger to death in my life. Instead, help me to put on patience and love each day. I need Your help to do this since I can't do it on my own. Help me to live in my true identity of being chosen and holy. Amen."

Day 10: The Patient Mom

~ Read: 1 Timothy 4:1-8 ~

"Preach the word; be ready in season and out of season; reprove, rebuke, and exhort, with complete patience and teaching."
Romans 5:8

As a mom, often when you think of the word "patience," you think of interacting with your children in a calm, peaceful way. Or, you may think of the opposite . . . yelling at your kids when you've lost your patience. That said, there is another type of patience to develop as a Christian mom.

Megan is a mom dedicated to pointing her children to Christ. From the time they were young, she would read them Bible stories and talk about the beautiful world God made. As they grew a bit older, she was intentional to have family devotions and prayer time. She talked to them about biblical truths as she read to them from the Bible. As they became teens, she would be open to hard conversations. She made sure her children knew why they believed what they believed.

Megan is an example of patience in the spiritual formation of her children. It's not enough to only occasionally talk about God. According to Barna research, a child's worldview is formed during the time between 15 months and 13 years of age. It is solidified into their teens.

While today's verse isn't a "parenting" passage per se, it is a great reminder to be sharing Christ day in and day out with patience. Even if you face challenges along the way, continue to be faithful in the calling God has given you.

While it's not up to you to save your child, it is up to you to be patient as you share Jesus over and over. It's up to you to be faithful in teaching what the Bible has to say. It's up to you to show what it looks like to love and serve God. It is up to you to faithfully encourage your children toward Christ . . . and then trust God to do His work in your child. This requires you to be a patient mom.

Reflection Questions:

What thoughts do you have about patience as part of spiritual formation?

_____

_____

_____

How are you being intentional to grow your children in Christ?

_____

_____

_____

What is one way you can point your children to Christ in this season?

_____

_____

_____

Prayer:

"Heavenly Father, help me to be patient in the years that it takes to invest in the spiritual formation of my children. I realize that I can't save my children, but I am called to be faithful to teach them Your ways. Help me to not be lazy, but to give my all in training my children in this most important area as You draw them to You. Amen."

Joy in the Journey

Joy comes from Christ

Day 11: The Fruit of Joy

~ Read: Galatians 5:22-23; 1 Thessalonians 5:12-24 ~

"Give thanks in all circumstances; for this is the will of God in Christ Jesus for you."
1 Thessalonians 5:18

Have you ever met someone who always seems to have a smile on their face? It doesn't seem to matter the time of day, the season, or the situation. They are always joyful!

Usually, we are drawn to people like that. You know, drawn to that friend who always has something nice to say to you. Drawn to the woman whose face lights up when she sees you. Drawn to those who are thankful in every situation.

Galatians 5:22-23 lists the fruit of the Spirit. These are things that grow in us as we grow in Christ. Joy is one of these. In fact, it is the second one listed.

In our key verse for today, you will see that we are to give thanks in all situations. It can be incredibly hard to give thanks if you're sad and depressed, right? Giving thanks helps bring about that joy. It helps you find joy in challenging situations, which we'll talk about more in this section.

Meanwhile, for today, how can you find joy in the day-to-day situations you find yourself in? When the baby is crying because he's hungry, but you're dealing with a toddler tantrum, where can you find joy? Sometimes it's hard, but there's always something. For example, your children are healthy enough to know what they want . . . or you're reminded that God is teaching you great lessons through these challenges, and He is with you.

The season of young children doesn't last forever, but the lessons you learn and how you exhibit joy will be of lasting value. Your children will learn from your example, and you will have learned to find joy in all circumstances.

Reflection Questions:

Who do you know that is always joyful?

_____

_____

How are you doing in the joy department?

_____

_____

_____

How can you find joy each day?

_____

_____

_____

_____

Prayer:

"Lord, I truly admire those who seem to be joyful all the time. I find it hard sometimes to find joy in the challenging seasons of motherhood. Please grow the fruit of joy in my life. Show me all the reasons I have to have true joy in You. Amen."

Day 12: Plugging Into the Source

~ Read: John 15:1-17 ~

"If you keep my commandments, you will abide in my love, just as I have kept my Father's commandments and abide in his love. These things I have spoken to you, that my joy may be in you, and that your joy may be full."
John 15:10-11

I love John 15. I've loved it for years, but my word of the year for 2024 is ABIDE, so it's taken on an all-new meaning. As you can see, it's scattered everywhere throughout this passage.

As a young mom, I realized that I couldn't do this motherhood thing in my own strength. I knew I needed God's help, so I prioritized time with God each day. Most of the time, I planned it for when I was nursing or the littles were napping. It didn't always work, but most days I could make it happen. That time would reorient my life to His.

Do you know what happens when you abide in Christ and His love? You become more like Him. You bear spiritual fruit in your life. You find deep joy and fulfillment in your relationship with Christ. As you are plugged into the Source, you will carry that joy into all aspects of life. You may even hear people comment about it sometimes—that they can see the joy on your face!

Sometimes, however, we let ourselves become unplugged from the source . . . from Christ. This happened to me recently. I was still in His Word each day, but I wasn't truly living in His strength. I was so busy striving instead of abiding that I was losing the joy in what God had called me to do. I was too busy *doing*.

Do you know what happened? God pruned me. He took away most of what I was striving to achieve. He showed me that without Him I can accomplish *nothing*. He helped me to realize that when I abide in Him, the fruit follows. And just like with pruning a favorite tree or rose bush, there are some rough edges because of it. Yet as you probably know, it's worth it in the next season.

As I abide in Christ, I find joy in what He has called me to do. I find joy in the tasks of motherhood. I find joy in my family. I want you to share in His joy, too!

31

Reflection Questions:

How would you say you are plugged into the Source? Into Christ?

_____

_____

_____

What happens when you start living in your own power?

_____

_____

_____

How has abiding in Christ brought you joy?

_____

_____

_____

Prayer:

"Dear Lord, it's so easy to start living life in my own power . . . to start striving. I realize that I will have joy to the full only when I abide in You. Help me to do that. Help me to prioritize my relationship with You above all else. In Jesus's Name I pray, Amen."

Day 13: Joy in the Hard

~ Read: James 1:2-4; Acts 16:16-40 ~

"Count it all joy, my brothers, when you meet trials of various kinds, for you know that the testing of your faith produces steadfastness."
James 1:2-3

Trusting God and finding joy in the hard, during the difficult times, can change even the worst of circumstances! I know sometimes it doesn't feel like it, but did you read the story of Paul and Silas in Acts 16 listed above?

Paul and Silas had been beaten and put in the inner prison with their feet in stocks . . . all because they had cast a demon out of a girl, causing her owners to lose income. This was a terrible situation, but Paul and Silas chose to sing hymns and pray, giving the situation to God. While the passage doesn't specifically say they were thankful, you can see their faith and trust in God.

God provided a miraculous earthquake, which freed them from their bonds. The joy and faith of Paul and Silas during this event led to the conversion of the jailer and his whole family, all because Paul and Silas trusted God with their hard situation.

Our verse today reminds us to count it all joy when we go through hard times. Paul and Silas were a much better example than I often am. They were praising God and praying to Him, even in the hard times, instead of complaining or trying to find a way out of it. Guilty!

While we never enjoy difficult situations, these situations are what grow us as a person. They cause us to depend on God more. Trials also can point those around us to God as we lean on Him.

I know I wouldn't be who I am today if I hadn't experienced the loss of my twins or the many moves and deployments. God has used all the hard things in my life to train me to trust Him. In Him, I can find joy in the hard.

Reflection Questions:

What stood out to you from the story of Paul and Silas?

_____

_____

_____

What is your first reaction when challenges come?

_____

_____

_____

How can you find joy, even in the hard times?

_____

_____

_____

Prayer:

"Dear Father, help me to find joy in the challenges of life. Help me to trust in You to lead me through it, even though it's hard. Use me to point others to You in my difficult seasons. Amen."

Day 14: The Source of Joy

~ Read: Psalm 16:1-11 ~

"You make known to me the path of life; in your presence there is fullness of joy; at your right hand are pleasures forevermore."
Psalm 16:11

I began to put items in a donation box. "Does this spark joy?" is what minimalist guru, Marie Kondo, says you should ask for each item you own. If it doesn't, it's time to get rid of it. I had way too many things to keep up with, so it was time to minimize.

The problem is, joy isn't found in our stuff or lack thereof. . . at least not true joy. If it was, we would all be happier. In fact, studies show that in countries where people live simple lives, they are happier in general.

Yes, there is a difference between happiness and joy. Happiness tends to be attached to our emotions. It's more outward and connected with an event, whereas joy comes from within. Joy is from the heart and soul. Joy transcends circumstances. Joy runs deep and leads to peace and contentment.

The materialism of our society claims that we'll be happier with a nice house, the latest tech, a successful career, or an extravagant vacation. We'll be happier if we are involved in x,y, or z. Yet, do these things ever satisfy?

Psalm 16 reminds us of our source of joy. Hint, it's not your house or even your family. In fact, David says that our fullness of joy comes from the Lord. Chasing after material things will only bring sorrow, but in the Lord, there are pleasures forevermore!

As you realize where your true source of joy is found, you can be joyful in the busyness of taking care of little ones. You can find joy in the exhausting days as you treasure the gift of pointing your children to Christ. You can rejoice that you are walking through this life with God. You can begin to notice the little moments that bring great joy, when you are seeing your children through the eyes of the Lord.

Reflection Questions:

Describe the difference between happiness and joy.

_____

_____

_____

What joy do you have that comes from a relationship with God?

_____

_____

_____

_____

How can you focus more on the joy you have in the midst of motherhood?

_____

_____

_____

_____

Prayer:

"Dear Heavenly Father, sometimes I get distracted by what the world says that I need. This doesn't bring joy though. I realize that true joy only comes from You. Thank you that in Your presence I have fullness of joy and pleasures forevermore! Amen."

Day 15: Gratitude Brings Joy

~ Read: Nehemiah 12:27-43 ~

"And at the dedication of the wall of Jerusalem they sought the Levites in all their places, to bring them to Jerusalem to celebrate the dedication with gladness, with thanksgivings and with singing, with cymbals, harps, and lyres."
Nehemiah 12:27

My Bible study group recently went through the book of Nehemiah. If you're not familiar with it, let me give you a bit of a summary.

Nehemiah was an Israelite captive in Babylon, who served as a cupbearer to the king. He was heartbroken when he heard that the walls of Jerusalem were in shambles. When the king inquired why he was so sad, Nehemiah told him. The king permitted Nehemiah to return to Jerusalem to rebuild the wall. He also gave him letters of permission to pass through the land, along with supplies!

Upon Nehemiah's return to Jerusalem, he rallied the people to rebuild the walls. A few leaders of the surrounding land tried to cause trouble and thwart their efforts many times. There was even a time when the men would build with one hand with a weapon in the other!

Finally, the walls were finished! At the end of Nehemiah, there came a time to celebrate and dedicate the walls of Jerusalem. The people were so thankful, which brought them great joy! You can read about it in our passage for today.

Motherhood isn't always easy. There are times of sadness when things are broken. There are many challenges along the way. Sometimes everything seems to come against you. Even so, as you choose to be grateful and celebrate the wins, like an amazing conversation with your tween, or hearing your words of advice repeated out of the mouth of one of your children, you will find joy in the journey. As Paul David Tripp says, "The DNA of joy is gratitude."

Reflection Questions:

What stood out to you from Nehemiah's story?

_____

_____

_____

_____

How do you tend to handle sadness and challenges?

_____

_____

_____

_____

What is something you can be grateful for today?

_____

_____

_____

_____

Prayer:

"Heavenly Father, Nehemiah and the people of Jerusalem went through so much to get those walls rebuilt. I admire the big celebration they had! Help me to find things to be grateful for, even in the challenging times. I see that gratefulness will bring joy to my heart. Amen."

Renewing Your Mind

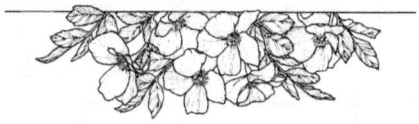

- *Day 16: Dangers of a Negative Mindset*

- *Day 17: How Can I Renew My Mind?*

- *Day 18: What We Should Dwell On*

- *Day 19: The Thankful Mindset*

- *Day 20: Be Like Jesus*

Set your

Mind

on the

Things

of the

Spirit

Day 16: Dangers of a Negative Mindset

~ Read: Romans 8:1-11 ~

"For those who live according to the flesh set their minds on the things of the flesh, but those who live according to the Spirit set their minds on the things of the Spirit. For to set the mind on the flesh is death, but to set the mind on the Spirit is life and peace."
Romans 8:5-6

William James, a psychologist who lived in the late 1800's, said "The greatest discovery of my generation is that a human being can alter his life by altering his attitudes of mind." Yet, the Bible had something to say about that way before then. In Romans 8, we see this very thing.

A negative mindset can affect all aspects of life. It can alter your perspective of life and hinder relationships. A negative mindset can affect self-esteem. It can cause worry and anxiety. It can even affect your physical health. While you may feel like you're alone, I read that 75-80% of most people's thoughts are negative! I found that quite surprising.

Mama, if a negative mindset is something that you're struggling with, the Word of God gives you hope. With God's help, you can change your mindset. That's what we'll be talking about over the next several days.

If you have time, go back and read our passage again. Setting your mind on the Spirit is life and peace. That is the opposite of negativity. Studies have shown that the mind cannot hold a negative thought and a peaceful, calm, or positive thought at the same time.

If you are living according to the Spirit, it will affect your mind. You live out what you believe, so if you believe in the things of God, it will affect your thoughts and your actions. Are you ready to make that change?

Reflection Questions:

What effects of a negative mindset have you noticed in your life?

_____

_____

_____

What have you learned from today's passage?

_____

_____

_____

What is one way you can live according to the Spirit this week?

_____

_____

_____

Prayer:

"Heavenly Father, I am struggling with a negative mindset, and I see that it is affecting my life. I know this isn't what You have for me. Help me to set my mind on the things of the Spirit as I live according to the Spirit. Help me to learn how to dwell on positive things. Amen."

Day 17: How Can I Renew My Mind?

~ Read: 2 Corinthians 10:1-6 ~

"We destroy arguments and every lofty opinion raised against the knowledge of God, and take every thought captive to obey Christ,"
2 Corinthians 10:5

"*I'm such a bad mom.*" "I'll never be good at this." "I'm overwhelmed. My life is a mess." "I thought this would make me happy." "I'll never look like that!" "Why don't my kids ever behave?"

Sometimes it seems that negative thoughts have hijacked our minds! There's so much information out there about the power of the mind. This influence works both ways. While our negative thoughts are powerful, so are our positive thoughts. As you'll learn over the next few days, what you think about matters.

Vladimir Savchuk says, "Positive thoughts are not going to stay, they need to be assisted. Negative thoughts are not going to leave, they need to be resisted. We must assist the Word of God by making room for it in our hearts, and resist the evil thoughts of the enemy by taking them captive and bringing them into submission to Christ."

This ties perfectly into our key verse for today. The negative thoughts and lies you are telling yourself go against the knowledge of God. They need to be taken captive and brought to the light for what they are. As you take these thoughts captive, you can not only see them for what they are (lies of Satan, the accuser), but you can trade them for God's truth.

Mama, though you walk through this life in the flesh, you are at war for your mind! Start by writing down common negative thoughts that you think. Name them for what they are. Next, find a truth from Scripture that counteracts that lie. Write it on an index card or sticky note and put it where you'll see it often.

This will give you a great start in replacing those negative thoughts! Tomorrow we'll talk more about what to dwell on instead.

Reflection Questions:

What negative thoughts do you tend to tell yourself?

_____

_____

_____

How can you combat those thoughts based on what you learned today?

_____

_____

_____

What are some truths from Scripture that you can meditate on instead?

_____

_____

_____

Prayer:

"Dear Lord, I realize that I have been dwelling on negative thoughts. I realize that I need to fight for my mind and take these thoughts captive. Help me to recognize these thoughts for what they are and replace them with Your truth. Amen,"

Day 18: What We Should Dwell On

~ Read: Philippians 4:4-9; Psalm 103 ~

"Finally, brothers, whatever is true, whatever is honorable, whatever is just, whatever is pure, whatever is lovely, whatever is commendable, if there is any excellence, if there is anything worthy of praise, think about these things."
Philippians 4:8

Jennifer sighed as she hung up the phone. She glanced over to the dining room in time to see her toddler hurl his spaghetti on the floor with a squeal. Down the hall, she could hear her four and six-year-olds fighting over a doll dress. Why was there always so much to deal with? So much to do?

I've talked to many moms like Jennifer . . . moms who feel overwhelmed and drained from dealing with their children's tantrums and fighting. These moms are facing endless to-do lists and keeping up with household responsibilities. They're struggling to maintain a sense of peace and joy in the busyness of raising their children. I'll bet you can relate as well. I know I've been there.

Kari Kampakis reminds us that "it's impossible to create a positive life while consumed with negative thoughts." Think about that for a moment. What you think about does make a difference in how you live your life. As you begin to look for the positive things each day, you will be more likely to notice positives the following days.

Yesterday we talked about taking those negative thoughts captive. Instead, you need to replace those thoughts with positive ones. Philippians 4:8 reminds us of what to focus on. Psalm 103 is another great chapter to read through and meditate on. In it, you can learn many characteristics of God and what He does for His people. We learn of His love and mercy, that He is forgiving and gracious, He keeps His promises, and rules over all!

Through intentional practice, Jennifer trained her mind to focus on things of Philippians 4:8. She made a conscious effort to seek out moments of beauty and laughter. She savored the small joys amid the challenges, even the spaghetti on the floor. Jennifer found that by shifting her mindset, she could experience true joy and contentment in what God had called her to.

Reflection Questions:

How do you relate to Jennifer's story?

_____

_____

_____

What stood out to you from the Bible passages today?

_____

_____

_____

_____

What one thing will you do this week to start focusing on thoughts from Philippians 4:8?

_____

_____

_____

Prayer:
"Heavenly Father, the busyness of this season is overwhelming me. I confess that my thoughts have not been focused on things that are true, right, and lovely. Help me to change my thought patterns and shift my perspective so that I can experience true joy and contentment in motherhood. Amen."

Day 19: The Thankful Mindset

~ Read: Philippians 4:4-9; Psalm 100 ~

"Do not be anxious about anything, but in everything by prayer and supplication with thanksgiving let your requests be made known to God. And the peace of God, which surpasses all understanding, will guard your hearts and your minds in Christ Jesus."
Philippians 4:6-7

Who in the Bible exemplifies thankfulness? There are a couple of people who come to mind for me. These include Hannah, David, Mary the mother of Jesus, and of course, Jesus. While facing even some hard circumstances, they were thankful to God and praised Him.

A thankful mindset gives the opposite results of what we talked about on Day 16 with the negative mindset. Thankful people are happier, more content, healthier, deal well with hard times, and have better relationships. That sounds pretty good to me! How about you?

The Psalms are full of David's thanksgiving to God. In some of them, he talks about the hard things he is going through at the beginning, but by the end, he is praising God. Psalm 100 is an example of a short but great psalm of praise to God.

Our key verse today reminds us to bring everything to God in prayer. Not only should you bring your requests to Him but also spend some time praising Him. When you lay everything at the feet of Jesus, His peace will guard your heart and mind. You will no longer need to worry since you are replacing worry with thanking God. How wonderful is that?!

In her book, *One Thousand Gifts,* Ann Voscamp tells of her journey to finding things to be thankful for in everyday moments. She began to list them. The more she looked for things to be thankful for, the more she found. I encourage you to give it a try. Maybe a thousand seems like a lot, but will you write down ten things you are thankful for today? Or just say them out loud!

Reflection Questions:

When you think of a thankful person, who do you think of? It can be one of the Bible characters I listed.

_____

_____

_____

What do you think about the difference between having a negative mindset and having a thankful mindset?

_____

_____

_____

How can you grow thankfulness in your life this week?

_____

_____

_____

_____

Prayer:

"Dear Lord, not only do You tell us to be thankful in all situations, it also has so many benefits! Help me to grow in thankfulness and give You thanks not only in the big things of life, but also in the little things. You have done so much for me. Amen."

Day 20: Be Like Jesus

~ Read: Philippians 2:1-11; John 13:1-17 ~

"Have this mind among yourselves, which is yours in Christ Jesus, who, though he was in the form of God, did not count equality with God a thing to be grasped, but emptied himself, by taking the form of a servant, being born in the likeness of men. And being found in human form, he humbled himself by becoming obedient to the point of death, even death on a cross."
Philippians 2:5-8

I don't think there's a better way to show how to be like Jesus than to revisit the story of Jesus from John 13. Jesus lived in a time when the lowest of servants would be the ones to wash the feet of others. Despite that, we see Jesus, the Lord of all, taking on this menial task. He washed all His disciples' feet, including Judas, who He knew would later betray Him. How incredible is that?!

I recently saw a real-life example of this. I go to a decent-sized church with many pastors overseeing different ministries. I was helping with snacks for vacation Bible school, but they were having a record number of kids attending. Do you know who helped? Most of the pastors were helping out at VBS all week. It was so touching to see the head pastor leading by example as he served those kids that week.

As moms, we are often serving our family. Yet, sometimes we get bitter about it. We feel that we deserve something better or deserve more time to ourselves. We wish we could be doing something more important. I'm here to remind you to lead your family by putting on the form of a servant. Be humble as you carry out the important calling of motherhood.

No one is asking you to physically die as Jesus did, but God does ask us to put others first. He asks us to forsake all for Him. He asks you to pursue His dreams and callings for you. Will you obey? He promises great rewards for our obedience to Him.

Reflection Questions:

What thoughts come to mind when you think of Jesus, the Son of God, doing a slave's task?

_____

_____

_____

How can you serve those in your family with a good attitude?

_____

_____

_____

_____

What examples can you think of of people who serve well?

_____

_____

_____

_____

Prayer:

"Lord God, sometimes I get bogged down in the service of motherhood. I forget what a good example You gave when you were here on earth. Help me to be humble and willing to serve in the way You have called me to do. Amen."

Priorities

In order to live intentionally as a follower of Jesus, it's important to know our priorities. Not only should we know what our priorities should be, but we should actually live by them. In this section, we'll cover the priorities of God, marriage, children, and caring for ourselves in a godly way.

Keep God First

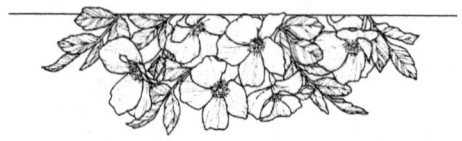

Day 21: But is He Really?

~ Read: 1 John 2:16; Matthew 10:38-39 ~

"And by this we know that we have come to know him, if we keep his commandments."
1 John 2:3

Like me, I'm sure you know people who say they're Christians, but you can't see anything about their life that shows that. They may say they prayed the "sinner's prayer" when they were a kid, so now they're going to heaven. Recently, I heard a quote during a sermon that stood out to me. The neighbor had said, "The only thing different about Christians is that they're busier on Sundays." How sad is that?

My goal for today is to reflect on what it means to truly have Jesus as **"Lord of your life."** Ask yourself, "Is He really?" 1 John gives us a test.

If you haven't already read the passages for today, please do so. I know when you're short on time, it's easy to only read the key verse. But, this is especially important. If you love Him, you WILL keep His commandments.

Are you willing to die to yourself and follow Him? Are you willing to do things His way? Are you showing that you have made Him Lord of your life by your actions? Do others see the difference in you?

It's so easy to get caught up in American culture, even "Christian" (I use that term loosely) culture. Except for going to church on Sunday, there may not be much difference between our lives and our neighbor's. Our kids take part in the same activities, watch the same shows, play the same video games. They may even be "nicer" or more hospitable than we are.

Mama, there should be a big difference in how we live as followers of Jesus. This world is not our home, and our future is in heaven! I'm guessing since you're reading this, you're heading in the right direction. The Christian life is a process, so let's keep following Jesus! Let's make Him Lord of our lives!

Reflection Questions:

How would you say your life is different from those around you? If it isn't, what is holding you back?

_____

_____

_____

What things have changed in your life as you pursue Christ?

_____

_____

_____

What is one thing you can do this week that will demonstrate that you are a child of God?

_____

_____

_____

Prayer:

"Heavenly Father, be Lord of my life. I realize it's a process, and I have so far to go, but help me to pursue You and not this world. Let others see that difference in my life. Help me to let go of the sin distracting me. Amen."

Day 22: Prioritizing Your Relationship With God

~ Read: Matthew 22:34-40 ~

"And he said to him, 'You shall love the Lord your God with all your heart and with all your soul and with all your mind.'"
Matthew 23:37

"I just didn't have time," I heard the woman across the table from me say. But you see, she wasn't the only one. In my years of attending and then leading women's Bible study groups, I've heard the excuse over and over.

The thing is, we *do* have time for what matters most to us. I often tell the women I coach that where you spend your time and your money will show you what your priorities are. You can say that God is important to you all day long, but does that show up in how you're living?

When you love someone, you desire to spend time with them. I know our relationship with God is often compared to a relationship with a spouse, but it's so true. If you never spend time with your husband or care about what he has to say, there are going to be problems in your marriage. There's going to be misunderstanding and hurt.

Today, I want you to take a look at your calendar. How are you spending your time each day? What do you do when the kids are in bed? Do you have time to watch your favorite TV show or scroll social media? What about time to call your best friend?

When we take a hard look at our time, we realize what is important to us. So, take a look again. Where could you spend some time in prayer? What about reading your Bible or reading a Christian book?

Right now you are in a busy season of raising children. Yet, I know that as you prioritize your relationship with God, you will be able to stay grounded and draw your strength from Him. The question is, will you prioritize it? By reading this, you're taking a great first step!

Reflection Questions:

How does my time reflect that God is my priority?

_____

_____

_____

What does my relationship with God currently look like?

_____

_____

_____

When will you spend time with God this week? Will you put it on your calendar?

_____

_____

_____

_____

Prayer:

"Heavenly Father, I say that my relationship with you is important, but I realize that how I spend my time doesn't always show that. I'd like to change that. Help me to be creative in spending time with You in this season. I want to love You above all. Amen."

Day 23: Growing in Spiritual Disciplines

~ Read: Colossians 3:1-17 ~

"If then you have been raised with Christ, seek the things that are above, where Christ is, seated at the right hand of God. Set your minds on things that are above, not on things that are on earth. For you have died, and your life is hidden with Christ in God."
Colossians 3:1-3

Several years ago, I went through a book on spiritual disciplines with some women from my church. I hadn't heard the term often before, but I've come to love it. In case you're new to the term too, let me explain.

Spiritual disciplines are habits practiced since biblical times to draw us closer to God. Spiritual disciplines include things like prayer and reading and studying the Bible. Meditating on and memorizing Scripture, fasting, and meeting with other believers are also spiritual disciplines. These are tools to help us grow in our relationship with God.

Spiritual disciplines are a great way for us to seek the things that are above as our key verses tell us to do. They change our focus, center us, ground us in Christ, and help us to become firmly rooted in Him. As we seek Christ more and more, others will be able to see Him through us.

While the spiritual benefits of these disciplines are the most important, there are also other benefits. For example, reading, studying, and memorizing God's Word can reduce stress (yes, please!). It can improve concentration, ease depression, and help develop empathy! Meditating on Scripture can reduce anxiety. Also, our children are watching. We are teaching them the importance and the benefits of reading the Word and spending time with the Lord.

Spiritual disciplines are important in the life of a follower of Christ. As you seek to draw closer to Christ, what disciplines do you need to develop? It's so worth it!

Reflection Questions:

What do you know about spiritual disciplines?

_____

_____

_____

How do spiritual disciplines help you seek the things that are above?

_____

_____

_____

Which spiritual discipline would you like to grow in? How can you make steps toward that this week?

_____

_____

_____

_____

Prayer:

"Dear Lord, I know I need to grow in some of these spiritual disciplines. They can each grow me in different ways. I want to seek the things that are above, so this is a great way to do that. Help me to make small changes toward You. Amen."

Day 24: But I'm Too Busy!

~ Read: Matthew 6:25-34 ~

"But seek first the kingdom of God and his righteousness, and all these things will be added to you."
Matthew 6:33

Dana groaned as she hit the snooze. It couldn't be morning already! Last night, she couldn't seem to fall asleep as her mind reeled from all the things she hadn't finished. She was certain she was failing her children. She wondered whether they would have enough money to pay the rent next week. It was too much!

As she dragged herself out of bed, she knew she should spend some time with God but decided she would do it later. Five minutes later found her sipping her coffee as she scrolled social media. Before she knew it, her three young children were awake and needing her attention.

Later that night, she fell into bed exhausted. *I should have spent some time with God today, but I was too busy,* she thought as she closed her eyes, hoping for a better night's sleep.

It's so easy as moms to think we don't have time for Bible study and prayer, well, other than an occasional "God, help me!" thrown out there. Truthfully, we can't afford *not* to spend time with God. It just may look a bit different in the busy season of raising children.

When my children were little, I often worked on my Bible study or did Bible reading while nursing a baby; sometimes at naptime. It was rarely in the morning because I was so tired then. Time with God could look like praying in the shower, leaving an open Bible on your counter, or placing verse cards around your home. It could also look like praying or listening to the Bible while you do the dishes or clean the bathroom.

As our key verse reminds us, seek God first. As you keep Him first, you will better be able to trust Him with the other details of your life.

Reflection Questions:

What excuses have you given recently for not spending time with God?

_____

_____

_____

What creative ways can you use to spend time with God in this season?

_____

_____

_____

What does it look like to seek God's kingdom first in your life?

_____

_____

_____

Prayer:

"Heavenly Father, I have been giving too many excuses for why I can't spend time with You in this season. I realize that I need to put You and your kingdom first before all the other things will fall into place. I know that You will take care of me and help me, so I don't need to worry. Help me to find creative ways to grow closer to You in this busy time of motherhood. Amen."

Day 25: Living "With" God

~ Read: Micah 6:8; Genesis 5:21-25; Hebrews 11:5-6 ~

"He has told you, O man, what is good; and what does the LORD require of you but to do justice, and to love kindness, and to walk humbly with your God"
Micah 6:8

It was a beautiful day. The sun was shining, and spring was in the air. As we walked down the street, my young children began running ahead. "Don't go too far ahead," I called out.

"We can still see and hear you," they replied. Now, you and I know that even though they can maybe hear you, you can't help them right away if they get too far ahead. You can't see if there's a car coming or comfort them if they fall because you're not *with them.*

Sometimes we're like this with God. *I got this, God.* We rush through life in our own way, not paying much attention to God. Yes, we may read a verse and say a quick prayer, but we're not really in relationship with Him. We then wake up one day and wonder why we're feeling so empty.

Just recently, I realized I was getting caught in this trap. I would pray each morning. I would read my chapters for the day. I would prepare for my Bible study. In spite of that, I was doing a lot of things in my life, including my business, in my own strength. I was striving instead of abiding. I was not doing it *with God.*

This year, I have committed to taking time to abide in Christ . . . time to do life *with* Him. I realized that I can't make things happen. I need Him to walk this life with me. Each day, besides my regular time with God, I have been seeking to listen to the Bible as I get ready in the morning. I have been trying to spend time in the afternoon to slow down and refocus my heart. Will you join me?

Reflection Questions:

What does a life *with God look like for you?*

_____

_____

_____

Do you tend to try to live life on your own strength? How?

_____

_____

_____

What step can you take this week to do life *with God?*

_____

_____

_____

Prayer:

"Dear Lord, I keep wanting to just run ahead through life, doing my own thing. I realize that You want me to go through life with You. Help me to really slow down and evaluate how to make this change. Help me to be a woman who walks with God. Amen."

Marriage

- *Day 26: The Godly Wife*

- *Day 27: Who Are You REALLY Serving?*

- *Day 28: Quality Time in Marriage*

- *Day 29: The Big "S" Word*

- *Day 30: Not on the Same Page*

MORE *Precious* THAN *Rubies*

Day 26: The Godly Wife

~ Read: Proverbs 31:10-31 ~

"Charm is deceitful, and beauty is vain, but a woman who fears the LORD is to be praised."
Proverbs 31:30

The "Virtuous Woman" of Proverbs 31 is famous. She is the pinnacle of a godly wife . . . someone we all aspire to be like. I'd love for you to take a look at some of her character traits.

This woman is trustworthy and hardworking. She is strong and industrious. The virtuous woman is generous and caring. She is dignified and kind. She is wise and well-prepared. Most importantly of all, she fears the Lord above all. I would say that because she fears the Lord, she is all those other things.

You may think that there's no way you can be like that. You think she is unattainable, but I would love for you to think about the story of Ruth. If you have time, go read her story in the book of Ruth.

Ruth was a Moabite woman who married Naomi's son. Yet, when Naomi's husband and sons died, she decided to head back to Israel. Ruth determined to go along and said that Naomi's God would be her God.

In Israel, Ruth labored, gleaning leftover grain from the fields, after the reapers finished their work of harvesting, to feed herself and Naomi. Her story shows that she had those character traits listed above. She even caught the attention of the field owner where she was working.

In Ruth 3:11, this is what Boaz had to say about Ruth. "And now, my daughter, do not fear. I will do for you all that you ask, for all my fellow townsmen know that you are a worthy woman." Some versions use the word "virtuous" instead of "worthy."

Ruth feared the Lord and it showed in how she lived her life. Dear Mama, put God above all and the rest will fall into place.

Reflection Questions:

How do you feel when you read about the virtuous woman?

_____

_____

_____

_____

How does the story of Ruth inspire you to be a godly woman?

_____

_____

_____

_____

What character traits do you aspire to grow in?

_____

_____

_____

Prayer:

"Dear Lord, I feel like I will never measure up to the virtuous woman, but I see that when I put You above all, You grow those traits in me. I'm inspired by Ruth as an example of being a virtuous woman. Help me to grow in You. Amen."

Day 27: Who Are You Really Serving?

~ Read: Colossians 3:18-25 ~

"Whatever you do, work heartily, as for the Lord and not for men, knowing that from the Lord you will receive the inheritance as your reward. You are serving the Lord Christ."
Colossians 3:23-24

Kayla sighed as she grabbed the laundry basket. Laundry was definitely one of her dreaded tasks. As she put the clothes into the washing machine, she mentally clicked through her tasks left for the day. Feed the kids lunch. Set up dentist appointments. Make her husband's lunch for tomorrow. Finish math with her nine-year-old. Clean the bathrooms. Take the girls to gymnastics. Make dinner . . . the list seemed to go on and on. It seemed that she was always behind and could never catch up. Why do I even do all this? No one seems to care, she thought.

If you're anything like me, you've also felt like Kayla. There's so much to do to keep your home running, and no one seems to care about all the effort you're making. Besides, with all your effort, it keeps getting messed up and you just have to do it again . . . and again. Over and over again.

Mama, it's time to remember something. You're not doing it because it has to be done. You're not doing it to keep your husband happy, although he may appreciate it. You're not doing it for your kids to notice. You're doing it for Jesus.

Colossians 3:23-24 reminds us of not only how to work, but why. We are serving the Lord Christ. What a privilege! We work hard for Him.

It's so easy to think we're serving our husbands, our children, our friends, and our neighbors. Rather, it's time to change that perspective. Serve the Lord as you do that laundry. Serve Him as you take care of your home and feed your family. Give it your all because you are serving the Lord Most High!

Reflection Questions:

How can you relate to Kayla?

_____

_____

_____

What would it mean for you to change your perspective on Who you're serving?

_____

_____

_____

How can you serve Christ in your daily tasks?

_____

_____

_____

Prayer:

"Dear Father, I sometimes feel like no one notices the hard work I put into this family. I realize that it's not about getting appreciation but about serving You. Help me to remember that I'm doing the work You have called me to and that it's You I'm serving. Help me to do my work for Your glory alone. Amen."

Day 28: Quality Time in Marriage

~ Read: Matthew 19:1-9 ~

"So they are no longer two but one flesh. What therefore God has joined together, let not man separate."
Matthew 19:6

As moms, we are so busy taking care of our families. We spend most of the day caring for our children and keeping the house from getting too crazy. Still, before there were any children, you chose a man, your husband. It's so important to prioritize your marriage relationship and spend quality time with your husband.

You may feel exhausted physically and emotionally from the day when your husband gets home. You may feel you can't do another thing for another person. Yet, your marriage needs quality time to thrive. Regardless of how you feel, it's important to spend that quality time in your marriage relationship.

The relationship with your husband should be your most important earthly relationship. As you know, any relationship needs time together for nurturing and growth. As our key verse reminds us, we are to leave our parents to cleave to our spouse.

Raising children is a part of what a married couple does, but that's not forever . . . even if it may seem like it right now when you're in the trenches! Quality time in marriage will bond you as a couple. It will increase your communication and satisfaction. It will even improve your emotional health. Quality time with your husband will also improve your health and decrease stress! Besides, couples who spend quality time together will be more likely to stay together through the hard times.

When your children are young, sometimes time together needs to be a bit creative. Find a time to connect each day. Be sure to listen well. Keep time together tech-free. Pray with and for one another. Plan regular dates (even if they're at home) and periodic getaways. Most of all, keep God at the center of your marriage.

Reflection Questions:

Are you spending quality time with your husband? Why or why not?

_____

_____

_____

What gets in the way of quality time together?

_____

_____

_____

What can you do this week to spend some time with your husband?

_____

_____

_____

_____

Prayer:

"Dear Lord, I'm so thankful for my husband, but I realize we need to spend more time together. Help us to prioritize quality time together in our marriage so it will continue to be nurtured and grow. Help us to keep You first. Amen."

Day 29: The Big "S" Word

~ Read: Ephesians 5:22-33 ~

"Wives, submit to your own husbands, as to the Lord."
Ephesians 5:22

Did you tense up when you read the title for today, not sure if I was talking about submission or sex? I'm not sure which is less touchy, but today we're talking about submission. There's a part of us that tends to be uneasy about submission. Ever since the Garden of Eden when Adam and Eve sinned, it became part of our sinful nature to not desire to be placed under someone else.

Today, I'd like you to put aside any preconceived ideas of submission. Be sure to read the whole text in Ephesians to get the big picture. Take a look at what the wife is to do and what the husband is to do.

Marriage is a beautiful thing when it works according to God's design. God is a God of order, so like a boss over the employee or a soldier under his commander, God has special roles for each marriage partner. This has nothing to do with one being better than the other. The fact is, there are many places in the Bible where women are exalted or praised.

In God's beautiful design, the husband will love his wife as Christ loved the Church and gave Himself for her. Wow! If your husband loves you like that, you can trust that he has your best interests at heart. He will take care of you and do what's best for you. He will ask you what you think before making a decision. He will lead your family in the ways of God. He will make it easy for you to come under him, submit, and respect him.

Sometimes, as you and I both know, our selfish and sinful natures get in the way and we mess up God's design. This makes it hard for us to submit or hard for our husbands to love. That said, as we draw near to God, we will also become more humble and loving toward our husbands.

Reflection Questions:

Prior to today, what thoughts would come up at the word "submission"?

_____

_____

_____

How does Ephesians explain how marriage works?

_____

_____

_____

_____

How can you grow in submission to your husband?

_____

_____

_____

_____

Prayer:

"Heavenly Father, I confess that the word "submission" tended to bother me. Yet, I see that Your plan paints a beautiful picture of marriage. Please help me to lay down my selfishness and pride and submit to my husband as the leader of our family. Help me to love and support him well. Amen."

Day 30: Not on the Same Page?

~ Read: 1 Corinthians 7:1-16; 1 Peter 3:1-2 ~

"For the unbelieving husband is made holy because of his wife, and the unbelieving wife is made holy because of her husband. Otherwise your children would be unclean, but as it is, they are holy."
1 Corinthians 7:14

Debra always felt a bit out of place at Bible study. The other women would mention that their husbands came with them to church or read the Bible with their kids. They would talk about serving at church together. Debra wished she had that, but she didn't.

Debra and her husband met at college. Debra had forsaken the faith of her parents and didn't even care that Tyler didn't believe in God. Still, a couple of years ago, she realized that she didn't want to raise her children without God. She started going to church and reading her Bible, ultimately placing her faith in Jesus for salvation.

Now, Debra and Tyler have a bit of a strain in their marriage due to their different beliefs. Perhaps you can relate. Or, maybe your husband is a Christian, but he's not leading your family as you think he should. Either scenario can be very challenging.

Our passages today remind us of what to do in these situations. Your husband is watching you. He can see if your faith is real or not. He can see the difference Jesus is making in your life. You don't know now, but your husband may come to Christ because of your example. He may be inspired to grow in his own faith.

When you are not on the same page spiritually, it can be challenging. Yet, with God's strength, you can continue to love your husband well. You can still enjoy a good relationship with him. You can still pray for him and be open to questions he may have. Remember, you are serving Christ as you live out your faith.

Reflection Questions:

How would you describe your spiritual walk compared to your husband's?

_____

_____

_____

What challenges do you have in marriage when it comes to your faith?

_____

_____

_____

How can you continue to honor your husband in this season?

_____

_____

_____

_____

Prayer:

"Dear Lord, I want my husband to know You like I do. It's hard when he just doesn't seem to get it or understand. Help me to be faithful to serve You as I love and honor my husband. I trust You to work in his heart and bring him toward You. Please bless him. Thank you that I can trust Your path for him. Amen."

Raising Godly Children

- *Day 31: Intentional Parenting*

- *Day 32: Building Relationships*

- *Day 33: Pointing Kids to Christ*

- *Day 34: Modeling For Our Children*

- *Day 35: Stay Strong in the Motherhood Journey*

Teach
Your
Children
Diligently

Day 31: Intentional Parenting

~ Read: Ephesians 6:1-4 ~

"Fathers, do not provoke your children to anger, but bring them up in the discipline and instruction of the Lord."
Ephesians 6:4

Ashamed and embarrassed, my face flushed as I realized they were right. Am I messing up my kids? Am I that bad of a mom?

We had gone camping with our three young children. As we were setting up, I was constantly telling my oldest two to settle down. I wanted them to stop being so crazy, quiet down, and quit going so far away. From the camp spot next to ours, I overheard the dreaded words, "I would hate to have her for a mom. She's been nothing but negative to her kids."

Coming from a group of 20-somethings, those words have been forever etched into my mind. I think of them when that negative or critical spirit comes out. I am reminded of them as I seek to now point out positive things my children are doing.

As parents, we have a high calling. What you do makes an impact on your children. When you are not intentional, you will tend to become lax or lazy in parenting. That was my mistake. I was pointing out all the wrong things my children did, but I wasn't intentional enough to show them the right way. I didn't look for the things I could praise them for. I didn't show them the right way to do things.

Intentional parenting is parenting that is deliberate and done with purpose. Intentional parenting is hard. It takes dedication, selflessness, and discipline. It takes a willingness to learn and grow. It takes humility to go to those older and wiser for help and advice. With that said, intentional parenting is worth it as you carry out what God has asked you to do. He will reward you for your faithfulness.

Reflection Questions:

Would you say you are an intentional parent?

_____

_____

_____

In what ways are you lazy in carrying out the call to bring up your children in the discipline and instruction of the Lord?

_____

_____

_____

How can you be more intentional this week?

_____

_____

_____

Prayer:

"Dear Lord, I confess that I have lost focus and have become distracted in parenting these precious children. Please forgive me. Help me to be intentional to raise them in the discipline and instruction of the Lord. Guide me as I point them to You. In the name of Jesus I pray, Amen."

Day 32: Building Relationships

~ Read: Hebrews 12:3-11 ~

"It is for discipline that you have to endure. God is treating you as sons. For what son is there whom his father does not discipline?"
Hebrews 12:7

As moms, we are all different and may tend to put more focus on some things rather than other things. In doing this, some of us tend to focus on the rules. We are often telling our children what they should or should not be doing. We tend to be critical of negative behavior and forget to praise the good. We might forget that we also need to build relationships with our children.

Josh McDowell says, "Rules without relationship lead to rebellion." I mean, how often do you hear of teens or young adults cutting off their parents? They no longer want to follow the rules but are pursuing the kind of lifestyle they want instead. Their parents try to point out the wrong, but the child no longer has any desire to listen or even be around them.

This is not to say that if your child rebels you didn't have a relationship with them. Each child eventually makes their own choices, which may even change in time. What I *am* saying is that your relationship with your child matters. It needs to come before the rules. Relationships over rules.

As you build a relationship with each of your children, they see that you care about them as a person. They see that you only want what's best for them. When they know that you are interested in them and care about them individually, they will be more likely to listen to what you have to say. They will know that the rules are in place to protect them.

Think about it this way. People who aren't followers of Jesus think Christianity is only a bunch of rules telling you what you can and can't do. By contrast, when you do have a relationship with Jesus, you see that all His "rules" are in place to protect you . . . and come from a place of love. This is exactly what we need to do with our children.

Reflection Questions:

Do you tend to focus more on the rules instead of relationships? If so, how?

_____

_____

_____

Why is building a relationship with your children important?

_____

_____

_____

What is one way you can grow the relationship with your child this week?

_____

_____

_____

_____

Prayer:

"Dear Father, I know how much You love me and protect me with your rules. Help me to grow the relationships with each one of my children. I want them to always know they can talk to me, even if they mess up the rules. Help them to see the rules are in place for their good and protection. Ultimately, help me to point them to You. Amen."

Day 33: Pointing Kids to Christ

~ Read: Deuteronomy 6:1-25 ~

"You shall teach them diligently to your children, and shall talk of them when you sit in your house, and when you walk by the way, and when you lie down, and when you rise."
Deuteronomy 6:7

What does diligently teaching your children the ways of God look like? According to Barna Research, about 68% of Americans claim to be Christians. Of that 68%, only about 9% hold a biblical worldview, and only 2% of parents! I find these statistics staggering.

As a whole, Christian parents are not doing their job. Yet, that does not have to be the case for you. Yes, pointing your children to Christ and teaching them what the Bible says takes determination. Modeling what Christianity looks like in day-to-day life takes dedication and intentionality. It's hard work.

Today, I encourage you to prioritize the spiritual formation of your children. It won't magically happen if you don't make a plan. How will you go about teaching them about God and the Bible?

Since worldview starts forming by fifteen to eighteen months of age, it's never too early to start reading Bible stories and talking about God throughout the day. As your children grow, take our passage for today to heart. Read through the Bible with them, teach them core doctrines, and share why you believe what you believe. Share the good news of the gospel with them over and over.

Talking about God can happen throughout the day as you deal with behavioral issues. Proclaim His wonder as you point out a spectacular sunset or revel in a cool scientific discovery. Yet, there also needs to be time for intentional teaching.

In order to be intentional, try a morning and/or evening devotional time. Use a Christian homeschool curriculum. Church services and other such activities can also reinforce the spiritual lessons you teach at home, but know they are not a replacement.

Dear Mama, I know pointing your kids to Christ is not always the easy way to parent. Yet, I know it is so worth all the effort!

Reflection Questions:

How have you been pointing your children to Christ? If you haven't, why not?

_____

_____

_____

How do you plan to prioritize the spiritual formation of your children?

_____

_____

_____

What can you do this week to point your children to Christ?

_____

_____

_____

Prayer:

"Dear Lord, I confess that sometimes I've been lazy about growing my children spiritually and pointing them to You. Please help me to prioritize teaching them about You and Your Word. Help me to teach them and lead them throughout each day. Give me wisdom in this area. In Christ's name I pray, Amen."

Day 34: Modeling For Our Children

~Read: Deuteronomy 4:1-14 ~

"Only take care, and keep your soul diligently, lest you forget the things that your eyes have seen, and lest they depart from your heart all the days of your life. Make them known to your children and your children's children—"
Deuteronomy 4:9

"Practice what you preach." "Live out your faith." "Do as I say, not as I do." We've all heard these conflicting statements. Yet, most things you read about raising godly children bring up one thing - the importance of modeling true Christianity to our children.

Last year I read the book *Raising Spiritual Champions* by George Barna. As I mentioned yesterday, according to research, more than 9 out of 10 parents do NOT have a biblical worldview. This means that they don't always filter life through the Bible as being the ultimate truth.

If this is the case, how can you pass on to your children what you do not have? How can you model what God teaches? A favorite quote from the book is "You do what you believe." You can say you believe one thing but live differently. Our children are smart and pick up on that.

Our children are always learning from us. They learn little things like how to get dressed, how to make a sandwich, and how to look both ways before crossing the street. They also learn how to interact with others, how to apologize, and how to be kind. Why would we think they won't follow our example in how we treat our relationship with God? They see the priority we do or don't place on it and His Word.

As a mom, you need to live out what you're teaching your children in easily noticeable ways. Let them see you spending time in the Bible. Let them hear you pray. Yes, you will mess up, but that's where modeling asking for forgiveness comes in. Our kids need to see real, authentic faith.

Reflection Questions:

How important do you think it is to model Christianity to your children?

_____

_____

_____

What are some ways you are modeling your faith?

_____

_____

_____

What are some ways you could improve on living out your faith?

_____

_____

_____

Prayer:

"Heavenly Father, I confess that I don't live out my faith as well as I'd like. I realize that I need to really know Your Word and put it into practice if I'm going to pass that down to my children. Help me to show my children what it looks like to love You above all else. Amen."

Day 35: Stay Strong in the Motherhood Journey

~ Read: Isaiah 41:1-13 ~

"Fear not, for I am with you; be not dismayed, for I am your God; I will strengthen you, I will help you, I will uphold you with my righteous right hand."
Isaiah 41:10

Practicing biblical motherhood is not for the faint of heart. When your children are young or still at home, they take so much out of you. You seem to be busy all day but accomplish nothing. You wonder how you can keep this up for eighteen years.

One of my friends would often say, "The days are long, but the years are short." While it may not seem that way right now, it's so true. I remember those years of sleepless nights. I remember the days full of keeping up with little ones and trying to not drown in household tasks.

Raising godly children isn't a sprint but rather a marathon. It takes time, dedication, intentionality, and strength. Isaiah 41 is a great chapter to remind you of where your strength for the journey lies. God is with you every step of the long venture. He helps you and guides you. He is the supporting framework that keeps you strong through the busyness.

When you are weary, be sure to lean on God for strength. It is His strength that is made perfect in weakness. Take the time to remember what He says about the value of a mother. Consider the valuable impact that a mother has in pointing her children to Christ. Remind yourself that your children are looking to you.

Now that I have an nineteen-year-old, I know how true it is that time flies by. I vividly remember when she was placed in my arms. I didn't know what in the world I was doing. Now she is pursuing her own relationship with God and is poised to launch into adulthood. The others are coming up right behind her.

Stay strong, Mama! Stay strong in Christ. It's so worth it! He is right there beside you every step of the way.

Reflection Questions:

How are you feeling in the motherhood journey? Are you weary?

_____

_____

_____

Are you drawing your strength from the Lord? If so, how? If not, why not?

_____

_____

_____

What truths can you remind yourself of when you are weary?

_____

_____

_____

Prayer:
"Dear Lord, I didn't realize how draining motherhood would be. I'm thankful for the reminder that this is an important calling, and that I can draw my strength from You. Please continue to uphold and guide me. Amen."

Rest and Self-Care

Glorify

GOD

IN

Your

BODY

Day 36: The Truth About Rest

~ Read: Genesis 2:1-3; Exodus 20:8-11; Mark 2:23-28 ~

"And he said to them, 'The Sabbath was made for man, not man for the Sabbath.'"
Mark 2:27

All the way back in Genesis you will find the beginning of Sabbath. God created the world in six days, but what did He do on day seven? He rested. He's God, so He wasn't tired. He was setting up a rhythm that would become part of Israel's way of living.

The word Sabbath means "to stop." It is to be a day of rest. In fact, the instruction to remember the Sabbath and keep it holy is one of the Ten Commandments. Back in Jesus's day, the Israelites were very strict about it. Practicing Jews still are today. No work at all on that day.

In Mark 2, Jesus reminded the Pharisees about the purpose of the Sabbath. He said it was for man. God created that day of rest for us. In our current culture, we tend to forget that.

We are busy, busy, busy. We can't take a day off or we'll be behind . . . or so we think. Actually, it has been found that we're more productive when we have rest. God has designed this day of rest to fill us back up, most of all, in Him.

Yes, I know that when you have little ones, you may not get total rest. Yet, it is possible to minimize extra work on that day, which is what I do. Keep it to a bare minimum by planning ahead to heat up leftovers or a frozen pizza on this day, or by doing household tasks throughout the week. According to John Mark Comer in *The Ruthless Elimination of Hurry,* ask yourself if the task is worship or rest. If not, don't do it.

I encourage you to ask yourself how you can practice Sabbath rest in your life. What kinds of things could you do on that day to draw closer to God, rest, and connect with those you love? It's not about the rules but about God's heart.

Reflection Questions:

What is Sabbath rest to you?

_____

_____

_____

What are your thoughts on Sabbath being for us?

_____

_____

_____

What will you do this week to open up Sabbath rest time?

_____

_____

_____

Prayer:

"Heavenly Father, I haven't even really thought about Sabbath rest. Please show me Your heart for this. I want to have a day to reconnect with You, rest, and connect with my loved ones. I want to be refreshed and ready for a new week. Show me what that looks like. Amen."

Day 37: Take Care of Your Body

~ Read: Mark 6:30-56 ~

"And he said to them, "Come away by yourselves to a desolate place and rest a while." For many were coming and going, and they had no leisure even to eat."
Mark 6:31

As moms, it's easy to get busy taking care of everything. You take care of your children, the house, your husband. You run errands and homeschool. But maybe you don't take care of yourself. You might not eat well during the day but then binge in the evenings because you're hungry. Do you stay up way too late because it's actually quiet then (ask me how I know!)? You don't have time to get the exercise you know you should get.

Sometimes you think you're doing pretty well with taking care of yourself, but you might start noticing weird symptoms. That's what happened to me. I started getting terrible, itchy rashes. After time and tests, I finally found out that my body was holding onto stress. My cortisol, the stress hormone, was high all day long.

Now, this isn't a health book, but as moms, we know we can't take good care of our family if we're depleted. Not only do the tasks of motherhood drain us, but pregnancy drains nutrients from your body. With depleted energy, you will be exhausted, grumpy, and less likely to put in the hard work of intentionally raising your children.

In our passage today, the disciples had been out sharing the good news of Jesus. Crowds were following them everywhere. They didn't have the time to rest or eat. Jesus told them to get away and enjoy some rest. He knew that physical rest was important.

We see that the crowds still followed them! Yet, Jesus took the time to feed them spiritually and physically. Then, He took time for Himself to get away and pray, which strengthened Him.

God will also give you the strength to do what He calls you to do, especially in the busy seasons. Even though He does this, it's still important to get away and enjoy some rest. Strengthen yourself in Him.

Reflection Questions:

How are you taking care of your body?

_____

_____

_____

Why do you think it's important for you to care for yourself?

_____

_____

_____

What is one thing you can do to better care for your body?

_____

_____

_____

Prayer:

"Dear Lord, I realize that while it's most important that I invest in my relationship with You, I still need to care for my body. I want to be the best I can be for my family. I want to have energy and feel well. I want to be rested and happy. Please help me to put the right amount of care into my physical health. Amen."

Day 38: Biblical Self-Care

~ Read: 1 Corinthians 6:12-20; Luke 5:16 ~

"Or do you not know that your body is a temple of the Holy Spirit within you, whom you have from God? You are not your own, for you were bought with a price. So glorify God in your body."
1 Corinthians 6:19-20

As Christian moms, we sometimes struggle with the idea of self-care. We might see it as selfish. We may feel that we're a better mom if we give up everything to take care of our family. I know I've struggled with this.

Yesterday we talked about the importance of caring for your body, but that's not the only thing that needs to be nurtured. Biblical self-care is about taking care of your whole self, especially your spiritual needs. Motherhood can be exhausting on all levels. Wouldn't you agree? Motherhood tries your patience and character at times.

Envision how you think about your children for a minute. You love them so very much. You don't want to see them sick. You want them to spend time with you and tell you their struggles. You want them to get proper rest. You want them to find their hope and their worth in God.

You are God's child. He wants you to run to Him with your needs. He wants you to feel supported by Him. He wants you to see yourself the way He sees you. He wants you to see yourself as loved and valued. He wants you to embrace your calling.

Biblical self-care isn't about extravagant care of yourself. It's about caring for your whole self in a way that honors the Lord and His calling for your life. It's about creating margin or space in your life so you can fully embrace this season. You can't carry out your calling if you're sick and exhausted. Nor can you carry out your calling to point your family to Christ if you're frustrated and snippy. Like many things, it's about balance. It's about being the best version of yourself. It's about honoring Christ.

Reflection Questions:

What thoughts does the term "biblical self-care" bring to mind for you?

_____

_____

_____

How does seeing yourself as God sees you change your perspective on self-care?

_____

_____

_____

_____

How can you honor God in the way you care for yourself physically, emotionally, and spiritually?

_____

_____

_____

_____

Prayer:

"Dear Lord, I struggle with the idea of self-care being selfish. I realize that I need to see myself the way You see me. I see that it's also about balance. Help me to honor You in the way I care for myself. Amen."

Day 39: Taking Self-Care Too Far

~ Read: Romans 12:1-2; 1 Peter 3:1-6 ~

"Do not be conformed to this world, but be transformed by the renewal of your mind, that by testing you may discern what is the will of God, what is good and acceptable and perfect."
Romans 12:2

She had been looking forward to it all week. Lisa slipped her feet into the warm water, leaned back in the chair, and let the stresses of the week drain away. She knew she had plenty of time before her hair highlight appointment. As her thoughts wandered, she thought about how she deserved this after her busy week.

In a society where moms are trying to keep up with the culture around them, they feel pressured to always look their best. We are told things like, "You deserve it." "You've sacrificed enough." "Is it wine o'clock?"

I had a conversation about this recently with a friend. We discussed that there is nothing intrinsically wrong with many of these things, but it all boils down to your heart. Why are you wanting to do things that level up your appearance? Why would we possibly choose to do things that only feel good?

Our passages today remind us that we are to be a living sacrifice and that we are not to conform to this world. 1 Peter reminds us that our beauty is not about the external but the internal. Does that fit in with how you're practicing self-care?

I love this quote by Danielle Forté, wife of NFL star Matt Forté. "The beginning of true self-care starts and ends in Him." How thought-provoking is that?

Take the time to meditate on today's Scripture. Talk to God about your ideas of self-care. Ask Him if you are glorifying Him in how you care for yourself as His temple. Are you taking self-care too far, or perhaps not far enough?

Reflection Questions:

Do you feel you're taking self-care too far? What about not far enough? How so?

_____

_____

_____

How can you glorify God in how you care for yourself?

_____

_____

_____

How do today's verses help you evaluate how you're caring for yourself?

_____

_____

_____

_____

Prayer:

"Heavenly Father, I want to honor You in how I care for myself. Help me to correctly evaluate the role self-care in my life. I want to care for the temple You have given me, and be beautiful because of who I am in You. Amen."

Day 40: For God's Glory

~ Read: 1 Corinthians 10:23-33 ~

"So whether you eat or drink, or whatever you do, do all to the glory of God."
1 Corinthians 10:31

Did you know that you can change a poopy diaper to the glory of God? What about the laundry, pushing your child on the swing, or taking an Epsom salt bath? These can be done to the glory of God as well.

For the past several days, we have been talking about rest and taking care of ourselves. I'd like to remind you that even in this, we can be glorifying God. In fact, the first question of the Westminster Shorter Catechism tells us that the purpose of man is to glorify God and enjoy Him forever.

While it may seem like it . . . and maybe you even act like it . . . your life is not about you. My life is not about me. It's about God and pointing people to Him. It's about glorifying Him . . . in everything. Life here is temporary, so we want to and need to make it count.

1 Corinthians 10:23-33 is a great reminder of this. In this passage, we find several things. First, we're reminded that not all things are beneficial, even if they're "lawful." Next, we are not to be seeking our own good but the good of others. And last, our key verse comes into play. We're to do everything, even the little things, for the glory of God. Why are we doing this? To point people to Jesus so that they may be saved and enjoy a relationship with Him forever.

So Mama, today I'd like you to reflect on how your life glorifies the Lord. How does your heart, your actions, your attitude and demeanor point to Christ? How does even your self-care glorify Him?

If you feel like you're not measuring up, you're not alone. We are all still a work in progress, including me. Thankfully, Christ in us will change us from the inside out. Are you willing?

Reflection Questions:

How can it change your attitude to realize that you can do day-to-day tasks for the glory of God?

_____

_____

_____

How can you glorify God in the way you rest and take care of yourself?

_____

_____

_____

What is one thing you can do this week to point someone to Jesus?

_____

_____

_____

Prayer:

"Dear Lord, I forget that You can be glorified even in the little things. Help me to glorify you in my daily life, including how I rest and take care of myself. Help me to be pointing others to You. Amen."

Live with Purpose

Many people drift through life. No goals. No meaningful plans. No purpose. I know that's not you or you wouldn't be here. You know that God has a plan for your life.

It's easy to go with the cultural flow, but resisting it takes intentionality, it takes knowing what God has called you to and consistently choosing to move forward in that. It takes planning.

In this section, we'll talk about the important resource of time, saying no to distractions, and keeping an eternal perspective. You'll be reminded that this world is not your home. Let's make our lives count!

Taking Control of Your Time

- *Day 41: Redeem the Time*

- *Day 42: How Should I Spend My Time?*

- *Day 43: What Does God Say?*

- *Day 44: Our Days Are Numbered*

- *Day 45: Make Your Life Count*

Redeem the time

Day 41: Redeem the Time

~ Read: Ephesians 5:6-21; Matthew 22:37-40 ~

"Look carefully then how you walk, not as unwise but as wise, making the best use of the time, because the days are evil."
Ephesians 5:15-16

I sighed, knowing my home was getting out of control . . . again. As I glanced around at the stacks of papers on the counters and the toys strewn around the room, I yelled at my three kids to come get their jackets on. We had errands to run, but my mind was on all the other things I had to do afterward. This was not the peaceful home and life I had imagined!

Have you ever felt like that? You are trying to keep way too many balls in the air, and you're waiting for them all to come crashing down around you. Do you ever feel scattered? That's how I felt. What I realized was that I was doing way too many things that I didn't need to do.

Our key verse reminds us to pay attention to how we're spending our time. I love the phrase "making the best use of the time." I wasn't doing that. However, I have grown in this area, and you can, too.

In Matthew 22:37-40, Jesus tells us what to focus on. We are to love Him with all our being and love others as we love ourselves. He says all the laws hinge on these. Is your time mostly spent loving God and loving others? This can revolutionize how you prioritize your time and decide what you need to let go of.

I know it doesn't seem like it when you're in the trenches with little ones, but this season will be over before you know it. Now that I have an eighteen-year-old, I can tell you that is so true! I encourage you to invest your time into the things that truly matter.

Reflection Questions:

What words would you use to describe your life as it currently is?

_____

_____

_____

What stands out to you from these verses?

_____

_____

_____

_____

What are your top priorities in this season of being a mom?

_____

_____

_____

Prayer:

"Heavenly Father, I realize I have way too much going on in my life. I haven't really been able to focus on the things that truly matter. Please help me to prioritize what You have called me to in this season. Help me to make the best use of my time for Your glory. Amen."

Day 42: How Should I Spend My Time?

~Read: 2 Corinthians 5:6-10 ~

"So whether we are at home or away, we make it our aim to please him."
2 Corinthians 5:9

Time management is another of the top struggles that moms tell me they deal with. Often we're involved in way too many things. Perhaps you are involved in a church small group, MOPS, or homeschool co-op. What about volunteering, kids' sports, and/or music lessons? This doesn't even account for grocery shopping, other errands, schooling, and house cleaning! It's no wonder we can't fit it all in.

Our passage today tells us that our life is about pleasing God. We're also reminded that some-day we're going to give an account to God for how we lived. This especially includes how we spent our time in this life. Yikes! But don't worry, a few small changes can really make a difference.

If you have some time today, I'd like you to grab a piece of paper. Set a timer for ten minutes and start writing down all the things you spend time on. If you need to check your calendar to remember, go ahead. Once you're finished, look over your list. Are these all things that help you prioritize loving God and loving those around you . . . or do they distract you from that?

Can I tell you that once I've removed things from my life that didn't fit in with God's priorities for me, I was better able to please Him with my time? I was able to be present instead of mentally focused on the next thing I had to do. I was able to have the space to enjoy time with God and my family.

How you spend your time tells a lot about what's important to you. Go back and look at that list you made. What things do you notice that may not be good uses of your time? It's time to eliminate them. Choose instead to only do things that please Christ during this time of your life.

Reflection Questions:

How are you doing with time management?

_____

_____

_____

How can the way you spend your time reflect what's important to you?

_____

_____

_____

What is something that you're spending time on that you have decided to eliminate?

_____

_____

_____

Prayer:

"Father God, I do not always manage my time well. I didn't realize how my time is often spent, until I looked at it this way. I see that the ways I'm spending my time do not always please You. Help me to change that. Amen."

Day 43: What Does God Say?

~ Read: Romans 13:11-14; Matthew 25:14-30 ~

"The night is far gone; the day is at hand. So then let us cast off the works of darkness and put on the armor of light."
Romans 13:12

Time is such an important commodity that we have been entrusted with, but often we tend to waste it. I'm reminded of Matthew 25, the parable of the talents. In this parable, the master goes away on a journey, entrusting talents to three servants based on their abilities. The servants who received five and two talents each doubled the amount. The last servant only received one talent, which he hid away until his master returned. When the master returned, he was happy with the two servants who doubled their talents. The last servant was condemned and cast out.

This parable is set in the context of several parables that Jesus told about His return. The talents are the different resources we have been given such as our time, abilities, and resources. We each have varying amounts, but how are we using them?

As moms, it's easy to get sidetracked by comparing our resources with the resources of those around us. We sometimes get distracted by wasting our resources. We may throw away time. We squander the abilities God has given us. We can throw away our money on frivolous things. I know I'm guilty of this!

This story serves as a reminder that God has given each of us resources to invest in His kingdom, whether it's time, talents, and/or money. He will return, and then we will each give an account to Him. Are you spending your time on the things God has called you to, or are you spending time on the things of this world?

As Romans 13:11-14 says, now is the time to put on the armor of light. It's the time to crucify the desires of the flesh and live fully in Christ!

Reflection Questions:

What did you learn from the parable of the talents?

_____

_____

_____

How are you spending your resources? Time, money, and abilities?

_____

_____

_____

What is one way that God is asking you to use your time for Him?

_____

_____

_____

Prayer:

"Dear Lord, I want to use my time and resources for Your glory and not my own. It's so easy for me to waste it on the things that don't matter. Help me to evaluate what changes I need to make in my life in order to use what I have for You. Amen."

Day 44: Our Days Are Numbered

~ Read: Psalm 90:1-17 ~

"So teach us to number our days that we may get a heart of wisdom."
Psalm 90:12

When people get to the end of their lives, do you know what they wish they had spent more time doing? Well, let me tell you that it's NOT working more, being busier, or holding a grudge. Instead, people wish they had spent more time with those they love and doing the things they love. They wish they had embraced their dreams instead of living up to the expectations of others. They wish they had given more, loved more, and been happier.

If you think about it, it's not that surprising. What *is* surprising is how often we forget that . . . how often we get caught up in momentary pleasures and worldly pursuits, how often we fall prey to the expectations of the world around us.

Psalm 90 is a great reminder that our time on this earth is short. Our time is like the grass that lasts only a short time. We are like a dream. Pretty sobering, right?

Even though our time is but a blip in eternity, it matters how we live it. What we do will either point others to Christ or turn them away. As we lead our children toward Christ, we are passing down the love of God to the next generation.

God has been carrying out His plan for thousands of years, and His way will not fail. He chose to use you to share His works and His power to your children . . . to grow His Church. How amazing is that?!

Reflection Questions:

How are you living life with eternity in mind?

_____

_____

What is distracting you from investing in what is most important?

_____

_____

_____

How can you intentionally point your children to Christ this week?

_____

_____

_____

Prayer:

"Father, it's so sad how often I get distracted from the things that truly matter in this life. I realize that my time on this earth is short. Help me to use it to point others to You. Help me to leave a legacy that continues long after I am gone. Draw my children to You. Amen."

Day 45: Make Your Life Count

~ Read: Philippians 3:1-21 ~

"Brothers, I do not consider that I have made it my own. But one thing I do: forgetting what lies behind and straining forward to what lies ahead, I press on toward the goal for the prize of the upward call of God in Christ Jesus."
Philippians 3:13-14

Who do you know who is a great example of following after Christ? What's different about them? How do they pursue Christ?

I have had several mentors over the years. I can think of two older women in particular who were so wise and pursued Christ with all their being. They knew Scripture well and could apply it in every situation. Even though I'm not currently near them, I aspire to be like them.

In our passage today, Paul was letting the Philippians know that it's all about Jesus. He reminded his readers that he was exemplary in following the religious rules and even becoming a Pharisee. Yet, that wasn't where his confidence was placed. Paul realized that his righteousness only came from Jesus.

This confidence led him to write our key verses. His past was behind him. He was moving forward in Christ. In fact, he was so confident in his path forward that he told them to follow him or others who were a good example.

I'd like to ask you again. Who are you following? Are they pointing you to Christ? Are they inspiring you to make your life count? As followers of Jesus, our lives are full of meaning and purpose! Let go of the distractions and make your life count for Christ.

Reflection Questions:

Who in your life points you to Jesus?

_____

_____

_____

If you don't have anyone, who could you get to know?

_____

_____

_____

How can you remind yourself to pursue Christ each day?

_____

_____

_____

_____

Prayer:

"Heavenly Father, I am inspired by _____. She follows you with her whole heart and I want to do the same. Help me to forget what has happened in the past and help me to move forward into all You have called me to be. Help me make my life count. In Jesus's name I pray, Amen."

Overcoming Distractions

- *Day 46: Satan's Tool*

- *Day 47: Wasting Time*

- *Day 48: Common Distractions*

- *Day 49: Subtle Distractions*

- *Day 50: Just Say "No"*

Say NO to Distractions

Day 46: Satan's Tool

~ Read: Ephesians 6:10-18 ~

"Put on the whole armor of God, that you may be able to stand against the schemes of the devil."
Ephesians 6:11

I don't know about you, but distraction is something I deal with on an ongoing basis. There's the ding of notifications, the lure of social media scrolling, and the to-do lists on both my phone and in my head. This doesn't even count the drama going on in the world around me. Can you relate?

Distraction is a common tool of Satan. I saw a quote to the effect that if he cannot have your heart, he will distract you instead. Sometimes, you won't even realize you're being distracted until it's too late!

Distraction keeps us from fully connecting with our husbands and children, spending time with God, and loving those around us well. These interruptions keep us from living engaged in each moment. They keep us from seeing the needs of those around us.

Since distraction is one of the schemes of the devil, we can use the armor of God to protect us from it. Put on your helmet to protect yourself from his lies. Use the shield of faith to block his attacks. Wield the sword of God's Word as your offensive weapon.

Distractions may be common, socially acceptable even, but we can rise above them. We can say no to distractions and intentionally live our lives instead.

Over the next couple of days, we'll talk about several different distractions we face as moms and how we can overcome them. It's only with the power of God that we can do that. It's with Him we can overcome the attacks of Satan, even distractions.

Reflection Questions:

What kinds of distractions are you dealing with?

_____

_____

_____

_____

How can you leave distractions behind?

_____

_____

_____

What would it look like to live your life without distraction?

_____

_____

_____

_____

Prayer:

"Heavenly Father, I realize how easy it is to be distracted in this life. I don't want to live distracted. I want to be intentional in how I live. Show me the distractions in my life and how to remove them or replace them with what pleases You. Amen."

Day 47: Wasting Time

~ Read: Psalm 39:1-13; James 4:14 ~

"O LORD, make me know my end and what is the measure of my days; let me know how fleeting I am! Behold, you have made my days a few handbreadths, and my lifetime is as nothing before you. Surely all mankind stands as a mere breath! "
Psalm 39:4-5

In our passages for today, we are reminded that our life is like a mist. It's here for a short time and then vanishes. In the grand scheme of eternity, this is so true, even though it doesn't feel like it in the long days of caring for littles.

Victor Hugo says, "Short as life is, we make it still shorter by the careless waste of time." While some wasted time can't be helped, such as being stuck in traffic or waiting at the doctor's office, we can be pretty good at wasting time on our own. We'll talk about some of these time wasters in the next couple of days.

Today, I want to focus on the reality that this life is short, and we need to make it count. The purpose of life is to love God and glorify Him. We are to point people, especially our families, to Christ. Satan loves nothing better than to distract us from that.

As you become aware of what is distracting you, you can focus on minimizing or even eliminating those distractions. Being aware is the first step. As you go throughout the day, pay attention to what you are wasting your time on, and write it down.

One thing that causes me to waste a lot of time is reading fiction books. Yes, it's good to have something you enjoy as a restful activity. Yet, I would get sucked into a good story, and it would take precedence over the things I should be doing. I would read instead of doing household chores. I would stay up way too late at night, causing me to be too tired to be pleasant with my children the next day.

Although I still love fiction, I rarely read it. I still enjoy nonfiction books, but they are so much easier to put down! Ask God for wisdom on what distractions *you* need to let go of.

Reflection Questions:

What thoughts do you have with this reminder of the brevity of life?

_____

_____

_____

What time wasters is Satan using to distract you from serving God fully?

_____

_____

_____

Are you ready to commit to overcoming distractions in your life? How will you change this over the next week?

_____

_____

_____

Prayer:

"Lord, I am here to love and serve You. It's so easy for me to forget and waste time with the pleasures of this world. Please help me to identify the time wasters in my life and let them go. Help me to use my time wisely. Amen."

Day 48: Common Distractions

~ Read: Colossians 4:2-6 ~

"Walk in wisdom toward outsiders, making the best use of the time."
Colossians 4:5

The average parent spends more time on their phone than they do with their children, according to studyfinds.org . . . like an hour more! While phones are a huge distraction, there are other common distractions as well. Social media, TV shows, shopping, and overcommitment are a few other examples.

As moms, it's easy to get caught up with these distractions. We follow the expectations and lifestyle of the culture around us. We feel oh so busy, get to the end of the day, and fall into bed, only to get up and do it all over again.

Our passage today reminds us to make the best use of the time. I think you will agree that the time spent on these distractions is not the best use of your time. Am I right?

What are we to be doing instead? According to our passage, we should be steadfast in prayer with thanksgiving. We should be looking for ways to uplift others and share the gospel with them. We should be making the best use of our time. How are you doing with that?

Don't worry, I'm not always doing great with this one either. Just the same, the first step is to recognize the distractions so you can cut them out of your life. Once you've done that, it's time to set up limits on those things and instead add things to your life that are in line with an eternal perspective. For example, trade scrolling social media for starting a gratitude journal, or instead of watching a show, play a game with your children or study a book of the Bible.

Reflection Questions:

What are your biggest common distractions?

_____

_____

_____

What are some ways you can cut back or eliminate this distraction?

_____

_____

_____

What is one way you can instead grow your relationship with God or share the gospel with those around you?

_____

_____

_____

Prayer:

Dear Lord, as I think about this, I am saddened by how much time I have been wasting with these distractions. I no longer want to go through my days distracted. I want to live intentionally for Your glory. Help me to use the time wisely in growing my relationship with You and pointing others to You as well. Amen."

Day 49: Subtle Distractions

~ Read: Matthew 6:25-34 ~

"But seek first the kingdom of God and his righteousness, and all these things will be added to you."
Matthew 6:33

When I stopped to consider how I wasted time in past years, here's what I noticed: I spent way too much time researching some healthy meals for my family. I spent thirty minutes trying to figure out what to wear since my closet was overflowing and most of the clothing didn't even fit. I needed to pay a bill, but I couldn't remember where I put it, so I spent about forty minutes looking through stacks of papers. Do any of these sound familiar?

Some of these things don't sound bad, but they are subtle distractions that affect your life. They either take your focus off of where it should be or waste your time because of disorganization. These subtle distractions keep us from using our time wisely.

Our passage today reminds us not to be worrying about what to eat or put on. Most of us aren't actually worrying about whether we have food or clothes period. Instead, it's so easy to worry about the kind of food we're putting into our bodies. Perhaps you are so overwhelmed by the chaos in your life that you do nothing. Maybe you worry about whether what you're wearing is stylish or making you look fat.

Subtle distractions such as worry, procrastination, disorganization, and learning useless skills will keep you focused on the here and now versus the business of the kingdom. They keep us earthly-minded versus heavenly-minded. Mama, we need to be seeking God's kingdom first.

I'm not saying don't ever put any thought into healthy food or nice clothes. What I am saying is to check your heart. Are these things taking up too much of your thoughts and time? Are they distracting you from loving and serving God and those around you?

Reflection Questions:

What are some of the subtle distractions in your life?

_____

_____

_____

How can you minimize these distractions throughout your days?

_____

_____

_____

How can you seek the kingdom of God first?

_____

_____

_____

Prayer:

"Father God, I confess that I have allowed these subtle distractions to keep me from seeking Your kingdom first. Please help me to honor You in my role as a woman and mother and keep these things in their proper place in my life. I don't want to be distracted from kingdom work. Amen."

Day 50: Just Say "No"

~ Read: Ephesians 4:17-32 ~

"And to be renewed in the spirit of your minds, and to put on the new self, created after the likeness of God in true righteousness and holiness."
Ephesians 4:23-24

"Can we please do the homeschool co-op? All my friends are there!" my daughter pleaded for the umpteenth time. Our local co-op was registering members for the next school year. While it offered some great electives, there were also other commitments involved . . . commitments I knew I didn't want to make.

In our current culture, there is so much pressure to have your children involved in sports, music, art, co-ops, clubs, and more. While some of these things may be good or even helpful, they are not ALL necessary.

Think about your top priorities in life as a Christian mom. Ask yourself if the activity is in line with your priorities. Is it helping you accomplish a goal you have? Is it drawing your children to Christ or distracting them from Him?

In our passage for today, the Gentiles, or non-Christians, have a totally different mindset than those who are in Christ. Christians are a new creation. What is important to the rest of the world shouldn't be to us.

Today, I'd like you to focus on what you can say "no" to in your life. What is distracting you or your children from the priorities God has called you to, right now?

Once you know what needs to go, it's time to back out of those commitments or activities. It's time to say no to future commitments. You can tell others that your calendar is full right now. God has great things in store for you when you have the space in your life to commit totally to Him.

Reflection Questions:

How is your life right now? Busy? Peaceful?

_____

_____

_____

What activities or commitments do you have right now that don't align with your priorities in this season?

_____

_____

_____

_____

What step can you take to make sure your commitments are in line with your priorities?

_____

_____

_____

Prayer:

"Dear Lord, I have been trying to keep up with the non-Christians around me, but I now realize that my life should be different from theirs. My life and my priorities need to be in line with what you have called me to do in this season. Help me to say "no" to the things that don't line up. Help me to be more intentional about what I allow into my life. Amen."

Eternal Perspective

- *Day 51: This World is Temporary*

- *Day 52: Too Comfortable?*

- *Day 53: Heavenly Value*

- *Day 54: Serving in the Daily Grind*

- *Day 55: Heavenly-Minded Mom*

Keep an ETERNAL Perspective

Day 51: This World is Temporary

~ Read: 1 Corinthians 3:1-23 ~

"For no one can lay a foundation other than that which is laid, which is Jesus Christ. Now if anyone builds on the foundation with gold, silver, precious stones, wood, hay, straw—each one's work will become manifest, for the Day will disclose it, because it will be revealed by fire, and the fire will test what sort of work each one has done. "
1 Corinthians 3:11-13

There's no doubt about it. Sarah was successful. At the insistence of her parents, she had worked her way through school and college, even obtaining her master's degree. She was doing well in her career but started to feel dissatisfied. As a mom, she realized she was missing out on so much of her kid's lives.

After much prayer and talking with her husband, Sarah quit her job to be home and home-school her children. God plainly showed something to Sarah. This world is temporary and true success doesn't come from achievement from a career. Instead, it's things of eternal value that will last. Sarah knew the impact she would have on her children by staying home. She knew time with them was worth more than the money she would make from working.

I realize that everyone's situation is different, and God has called us to distinctive things, but please don't miss my point. The main thing to consider is if the things you invest in have eternal value. When you stand before God, how much of what you invested in will line up with His will for you? Conversely, how much will be burned up?

Let's go back to Sarah for a minute. Her dad did not see the value of what she chose to do. He hinted that this was temporary, right? However, as Sarah pursued God, she knew she was making the right choice. She knew she was investing in things of eternal value. In the end, Sarah's parents were happy for her because they knew she was doing what she felt called to do.

Reflection Questions:

What temporary things are you investing your time into?

_____

_____

_____

What things of eternal value are you investing in?

_____

_____

_____

How can you remind yourself that this world is temporary?

_____

_____

_____

_____

Prayer:

"Dear Lord, I realize that this world is temporary but the things I invest my time into don't always show that. Please show me what I need to let go of in order to more fully pursue things of eternal value. Thank you! Amen."

Day 52: Too Comfortable?

~ Read: 1 John 2:15-17; James 4:1-10 ~

"Do not love the world or the things in the world. If anyone loves the world, the love of the Father is not in him."
1 John 2:15

You are in a war! I know it's easy to forget that, but there is a war for your heart. Even as a child of God, the world pulls at us constantly. Dwight L. Moody reminds us that "If I walk with the world, I can't walk with God."

1 John is very clear about what it looks like to be a follower of Jesus. Take a look at the key verse again. If you are all about the things of this world, the love of the Father isn't in you. In other words, you can't pursue the things of this world and God. They don't exist together.

As we'll talk about more in the following devotionals, this world is not our home. It's only temporary. However, our sinful nature still feels the comfort of the things of the world and draws us toward them.

Katy was a young mom who realized she was too comfortable. She spent her time bringing her children to mom's groups, shopping for the latest clothing and gadgets, and pursuing her dream of becoming an Instagram influencer. One Sunday, her pastor spoke from 1 John 2: 15-17. As she listened, the Holy Spirit began working in her heart. Tears began streaming down her cheeks as she realized that she was pursuing things that didn't ultimately matter.

Maybe you can relate to Katy. I know that some days I sure can! Are you realizing that this world has more of your heart than God does? Mama, you can change. Like Katy, you can run whole heartedly after God. Draw near to Him and He will draw near to you. He's waiting for you.

Reflection Questions:

Are you trying to walk with the world and with God?

_____

_____

_____

What worldly things have your heart?

_____

_____

_____

How can you draw near to God this week?

_____

_____

_____

Prayer:

"Dear Lord, the world has way too much of me than it should have. Help me to break free from the comforts of this world and draw near to You instead. I want You to have my whole heart. Amen."

Day 53: Heavenly Value

~ Read: Matthew 6:19-24 ~

"Do not lay up for yourselves treasures on earth, where moth and rust destroy and where thieves break in and steal, but lay up for yourselves treasures in heaven, where neither moth nor rust destroys and where thieves do not break in and steal."
Matthew 6:19-20

Emily was ready to make some changes in her life. During college, she had stopped going to church and instead made friends who made poor choices. Now, five years later, with a three year old and a one year old, she realized that she didn't want to do this mom thing without God.

What Emily recognized is that life apart from God is empty and meaningless, and she was tired of it. She noticed she was living her life for things that only had temporary value. She knew that she only needed to repent and turn back to God. She began praying again . . . and reading her Bible.

Maybe, like Emily, you have recently come to Christ (or come back to Christ). You are ready to stop living for the things of this world and instead live for things that actually have eternal value.

What are those things with heavenly value? Well, it's definitely not our stuff. The things that have heavenly value are the things we do for God . . . telling others about Him, loving others, obeying His commands, teaching and training our children about Him.

Our passage today reminds us that we can't serve God and money, or the things of this world. Those things don't last, but how we live for Jesus does. This is how we lay up treasures in heaven. Will you join me as we seek to live our life for things of heavenly value?

Are you laying up earthly or heavenly treasure?

_____

_____

_____

What things of heavenly value would you like to invest in?

_____

_____

_____

What is one thing you can do this week to invest in those things?

_____

_____

_____

_____

Prayer:

"Dear Lord, I am tired of living for earthly things. I realize that only the things with heavenly value will last. Help me to reevaluate my life and focus on things with lasting value. Help me to point those around me to You. Amen.

Day 54: Serving in the Daily Grind

~ Read: Romans 12:9-21 ~

"Love one another with brotherly affection. Outdo one another in showing honor. Do not be slothful in zeal, be fervent in spirit, serve the Lord."
Romans 12:10-11

Along with Colossians 3, Romans 12 is a great chapter to read to learn what it looks like to live as a true Christian. When you choose to trust in Jesus as Savior and Lord, it will make a difference in how you live. Romans 12 walks us through what some of those differences look like in daily life.

Meagan was a young mom of three children six and under. She was feeling overwhelmed by all the responsibilities on her plate. This was causing her to question whether it was worth it. She often thought about how much of a difference she could be making for God if she was still working her job instead of being with her children all day long.

Meagan began meeting with an older woman from her church, whom she looked up to. This mentor mom reminded her of how important it was to serve God exactly where she was. She reminded her of the difference she was making as she proclaimed God to her children.

Meagan began to see that she could live out Romans 12 in her home and community. She could love those around her well and show them honor. She could pray for others and help them as needs arose. She made it her aim to live peaceably with all, especially those in her family. Meagan finally saw that she could serve God in her everyday life as a mom.

Like Meagan, you can serve God in the daily grind as well. Just because you are busy caring for your children and your home doesn't mean you aren't serving God. You are a huge influence in teaching your children what it looks like to live out your faith practically.

Reflection Questions:

Do you feel that you could be doing more for God if you weren't so busy being a mom?

_____

_____

_____

What key phrases from Romans 12 most stood out to you and why?

_____

_____

_____

_____

How can the idea of serving God in daily life as a mom change your perspective?

_____

_____

_____

_____

Prayer:
"Dear Father, I often find myself so overwhelmed by all that I have to do that I forget that I can serve you in it. Help me to live out Romans 12 within my family and in my community. I want those around me to see You. Amen.

Day 55: Heavenly-Minded Mom

~ Read: 2 Corinthians 4:7-18; Colossians 3:2 ~

"For this light momentary affliction is preparing for us an eternal weight of glory beyond all comparison, as we look not to the things that are seen but to the things that are unseen. For the things that are seen are transient, but the things that are unseen are eternal."
2 Corinthians 4:17-18

Stephanie walked away from the park discouraged. As she pushed her double stroller, she thought about the conversation that took place among the moms there. The conversation bounced around so much. It covered things such as how important it was to feed your children real food. They talked about what activities each child participated in. They then covered why early education was essential. She knew she wasn't the only Christian mom there. Why did the conversations never seem to center on the importance of a child's spiritual development or what God is doing in your life?

Can you relate to Stephanie? I know I can. There have been many times throughout my motherhood journey when I wondered why Christian moms didn't talk more about these important spiritual truths . . . about how to focus on growing our kids in Christ instead of focusing on sports.

I may be stepping on some toes here, but it's so easy to forget the most important thing. This world is temporary, but eternity is not. This world is in our faces, so it's easy to let it distract us from focusing on heavenly things. Yet, as you focus on heavenly things, it will change what you do in the here and now.

Colossians 3:2 reminds us to set our minds on things above. According to 2 Corinthians 4:18, it is the unseen things that are eternal. The heavenly-minded mom will focus on how she can serve God in her daily life. She will desire to point others to Him and build up heavenly treasure. These are the things that will last.

Reflection Questions:

How can being a heavenly-minded mom make a difference in how you live out your life?

_____

_____

_____

What are some things around you that are distractions from that heavenly focus?

_____

_____

_____

What is one change you can make this week to become more heavenly-minded?

_____

_____

_____

_____

Prayer:

"Dear Lord, it's so easy to set my mind on the things that are right in front of me here in this world. I know that's not how You want me to live. Help me to become more heavenly-minded. I know this will change how I live out my life. Amen."

Leaving a Legacy

- *Day 56: What's Your Legacy?*

- *Day 57: What Kind of Influencer Are You?*

- *Day 58: An Eternal Impact*

- *Day 59: Just a Stay-At-Home Mom*

- *Day 60: Run the Race!*

Leave a **Godly** Legacy

Day 56: What's Your Legacy?

~ Read: 1 Peter 2:1-12; Psalm 102:18 ~

"Let this be recorded for a generation to come, so that a people yet to be created may praise the
Lord:*"*
Psalm 102:18

Have you ever thought about what kind of legacy you will leave? Often we don't think about it unless someone has died. Today, I'd love to challenge you to think about what kind of legacy you will leave, since this will affect how you live now.

A legacy is anything handed down from the past, like from a predecessor. Dietrich Bonhoeffer wisely said, "A righteous man is one who lives for the next generation." We see from Scripture that this is the true heart of God . . . passing down the stories of how He delivered His people from one generation to the next.

God's design for the Christian family includes passing on the priceless treasure He has given us to the children He has entrusted to us. We teach them to make their faith their own. If not, they may adopt some of the religious practices we teach them without having a relationship with God.

Modeling what a relationship with Christ looks like is so important for inspiring our children to follow in our footsteps. If they see a disconnect between our talk and our walk, they will pick up on the fact that our faith isn't really making a difference in our lives. This is not leaving a legacy.

Are you ready to leave a godly legacy? Are you doing your part to point the next generation to Christ and build His Church? As we do this, we are building an honorable culture that will last way after we're gone. We will be inspiring the faith of our children, grandchildren, and beyond. We will be living beyond the here and now of this world and for eternity instead.

Reflection Questions:

What kind of legacy are you leaving at this point?

_____

_____

_____

What do you want your legacy to look like?

_____

_____

_____

_____

What things would you like to change in order to point your children to Christ and leave that kind of legacy?

_____

_____

_____

Prayer:

"Heavenly Father, it's so easy to forget that how I live now can make a huge difference in the lives of my children, grandchildren, and beyond. Help me to really be conscientious of how I'm living in order to point those around me to Christ. Help me to leave a legacy that lasts way beyond me. Amen."

Day 57: What Kind of Influencer are You?

~ Read: John 15:12-17; 1 Peter 2:9 ~

"But you are a chosen race, a royal priesthood, a holy nation, a people for his own possession, that you may proclaim the excellencies of him who called you out of darkness into his marvelous light."
1 Peter 2:9

*"You **will** influence those around* you. The question is, how?" This question jolted me as I heard my pastor, Chris Johnson, ask it. As a Christian blogger who is active on social media, I knew that was what I was trying to do . . . influence other Christian moms to live with purpose. However, I really hadn't thought about how we are all influencing those around us in some way or another.

I have thought of that question often over the past several months. As a mom, am I pointing my children to Christ? Am I telling the other moms at homeschool recess about God? Am I loving my neighbors well? To be honest, I don't always do a great job with this.

According to our verses for today, we are to be proclaiming Christ to those around us. After all, He has changed our lives and brought us from darkness to light! We are to be showing love to those around us as we lead others toward Christ.

So, Mama, let me ask *you* this question. How are you influencing those around you? Take some time to genuinely think and pray over this. Are you guiding your family and others around you toward Christ or pushing them away from Him?

Reflection Questions:

How are you influencing those around you?

_____

_____

_____

_____

What do you think about the fact that you *do influence those around you in some way?*

_____

_____

_____

How can you be more intentional about influencing others toward Christ this week?

_____

_____

_____

_____

Prayer:

"Dear Lord, I didn't realize the impact I truly have on those around me. Help me to intentionally point my family and those around me to You. Help me to see the opportunities around me to share Your love and truth. Amen."

Day 58: An Eternal Impact

~ Read: Psalm 78:1-8 ~

"We will not hide them from their children, but tell to the coming generation the glorious deeds of the LORD, and his might, and the wonders that he has done."
Psalm 78:4

Donna is a mom who showed me what it was like to leave an eternal impact. After becoming a Christian as an adult, she embraced the call to love and serve God and others. She poured into homeschooling her large family, serving in her local church, and helping her neighbors and friends. She encouraged and inspired those around her.

As she grew older, she found great joy when her husband came to Christ. She mentored young mothers with her kindness and wisdom. Donna even counseled those going through hard situations to help them lean on Jesus.

I was one of many women who have been impacted by her example, and she has inspired me to do the same. While not all of us will impact many, we do have the capacity to impact those in our family and community circles. Simply by sharing what Jesus has done in our lives and by loving others well, those around us will learn of Him.

Psalm 78 is a great reminder to be sharing the wondrous deeds of the Lord. Asaph, the author, shares that by telling what God has done, our children will be inspired to put their hope in Him. I don't know about you, but I just want my children to put their faith and trust in the Lord. I want them to grow in their own relationship with God.

It's so easy to forget the big picture while you're in the trenches of motherhood, but keeping God's kingdom in mind will give you hope and purpose each day. It will keep you joyful and inspired to continue to love God and your family well.

Reflection Questions:

Who do you know who inspires you to live for eternity?

_____

_____

_____

How can it help you in the day-to-day to remember the big picture?

_____

_____

_____

What is one way you grow in making an eternal impact?

_____

_____

_____

_____

Prayer:

"Dear Lord, I want to impact those around me, especially my children, for eternity. Please help me to remember the big picture in the busyness of day-to-day life. I want to praise You to those around me. Amen"

Day 59: Just a Stay-at-Home Mom

~Read: Psalm 145:1-21 ~

"One generation shall commend your works to another, and shall declare your mighty acts."
Psalm 145:4

Can I share something with you? There's no such thing as "just a stay-at-home mom." Now, no matter what kind of mom you are, the point still applies. In our culture, the importance of motherhood is minimized. People want to know what you do besides being a mom. Culture puts all kinds of expectations on us, but they don't realize how significant our role is.

Let me tell you about a special woman who was "just" a stay-at-home mom. She was loving and kind. She and her husband always opened their home for whatever was needed – Bible studies, missionary visitors, someone who needed a place to stay for a while. She would leave a gospel tract wherever she went. She would cook and bake delicious food, breads, and treats for whoever was around. She faithfully read, studied, and discussed the Bible each day with her husband. She would hand out a yearly Bible reading guide to friends and family alike. She exuded love.

This godly woman died at 98 years old. Her funeral was packed to the hilt with those who knew and loved her. People spoke of the impact she made on their lives. It hit me. She was "just' a stay-at-home mom, but look at the impact she made! She was my grandmother.

John Wesley said, "I learnt more about Christianity from my mother than from all the theologians in England." Our role as moms is incredibly important. So, let's take our job seriously and point our children to Christ! Let's love and serve those around us well as we pursue Christ.

Reflection Questions:

Do you ever feel that you're "just" a mom? Why or why not?

_____

_____

_____

How are you encouraged that your job as a mom is important?

_____

_____

_____

What kind of legacy do you want to leave for your family?

_____

_____

_____

Prayer:

"Dear Lord, sometimes I feel that I'm not doing enough for You because I'm so busy taking care of my home and family. Thank You for this reminder that I can be faithful and impactful to those around me as I point them to You in daily life. Help me to be bold in sharing the gospel with those I come in contact with. Amen."

Day 60: Run the Race!

Read: 2 Corinthians 6:1-10; Hebrews 12:1-2

"Therefore, since we are surrounded by so great a cloud of witnesses, let us also lay aside every weight, and sin which clings so closely, and let us run with endurance the race that is set before us, looking to Jesus, the founder and perfecter of our faith, who for the joy that was set before him endured the cross, despising the shame, and is seated at the right hand of the throne of God."
Hebrews 12:1-2

As we wrap up this devotional, I'd love to encourage you to continue with endurance in the motherhood race God has called you to. Just like in the Christian life, you will face trials, sleepless nights, obstacles, losses, and more. Yet, let me remind you that you will also reap joys, gladness, rewards, and satisfaction.

The author of Hebrews reminds you exactly how to run this race. First of all, you need to set aside the things of this world that are weighing you down. We've been talking about many of these things. Then, lay aside any sins that are keeping you from being the mom God has called you to be.

Once you have left behind the weights and the sin, you can run with endurance. This is not a sprint, so it will take everything you've got. While this may sound exhausting, and it often is, looking to Jesus is what will get you through. He endured the cross so that He could perfect your faith. How amazing is that?!

Dear Mama, with the Lord as your strength, you have everything you need to be the mom God called you to be. He will give you strength when you have none. He will give patience when yours is running out. He gives wisdom to handle the challenging situations you face. He also gives joy for the journey. Hold fast to Him. He is always there to help you.

Reflection Questions:

How have you been running the race of motherhood?

_____

_____

_____

How can you run this race more effectively?

_____

_____

_____

What do you want to remember from this devotional?

_____

_____

_____

Prayer:

"Heavenly Father, I want to run not only the race of motherhood, but also the race of the Christian life well. Help me to lay aside the things that are holding me back and look to You for my strength. Give me what I need to run well for Your glory. Amen."

Now What?

Congratulations on finishing this devotional! I'm thrilled you have not only joined me for this journey, but that you finished! So, now what? Well, if you haven't already, I'd love for you to connect with me in my Facebook group, Christian Moms Living on Purpose.

Also, you can join my email list at https://mamareflections.com/. I offer encouragement, and more for those of you who are overwhelmed in the day-to-day of motherhood and are ready to make some changes!

If you've really loved this devotional, please share it with a friend . . . or 10! You can also gather some friends to go through this again as a small group. It's always amazing what we can learn from discussing with others. This is also a great way to build a mom community.

And last, if you are still new to Christianity or to spending time with God daily, it would be helpful to get involved in a local church if you aren't already. Also, there are some great devotionals, including ones for moms, in the YouVersion app. Growing in Christ is a life-long process. Galatians 6:9 is a great reminder to not grow weary in doing what God has called you to do. He will give you just what you need!

Small Group Discussion Guide

- What did you learn about God this week?

- What stood out to you from this week's devotions?

- Are you struggling with anything you read this week?

- What challenges are you dealing with that you need God's help for?

- What is one change you want to make this week based on this topic?

- How can you help someone else dealing with this issue?

- What is God teaching you this week?

- Which Scripture stood out to you the most? Why?

- How can we pray for you this week?

Acknowledgements

This work has been a labor of love for those who will read it. I'm thankful for my family for supporting my ministry, and I'm forever grateful to those who have tangibly guided me in this process. I'd like to thank my team and coaches at Kingdom Builders Academy for their support and inputs on my devotional. I'd like to thank Linda Geiger especially, for taking the time to thoroughly edit this work. She gave me such valuable feedback. Jade Lin-Parayil was also instrumental with valuable insights as well as weekly prayer during this process. I'm forever grateful!

My daughter, Alayna Niblack, helped me with cover fonts as well as designed the inside, making it so pretty. Lastly, I'd like to thank my beta readers and launch team. You have helped me make this possible as well as helping me spread the word. You are all so appreciated.